ALL ABOUT
HARRY

HARRY WARNER
BREAKING THE SILENCE

To Shazzy,

CASS WARNER SPERLING

Cass Warner

Library of Congress Cataloging-in-Publication Data
Sperling, Cass Warner, 1948-
The Brothers Warner / Cass Warner Sperling.

Paperback ISBN 978-1-960018-39-7

Warner Bros. Pictures-History. 2. Warner, Harry Morris, 1881-1978. 3. Warner,
Jack L., 1892-1978. I. Millner, Cork, 1931-2013 Warner, Jack, 1916-1995.
Manufactured in the United States of America.

Contents

For Grandpa. v

Who Was Harry Warner?. 1

The Beginning. 5

Dapper Harry 11

In Harry's Own Words 16

The End. 143

The Last Time I Saw Grandpa 145

Eulogy 147

The Warner Family 149

The Production Code 167

Acknowledgment 173

Cass with Grandpa

For Grandpa

In the 1950s there was no freeway to Woodland Hills near the city of Los Angeles. First thing on a Saturday morning our family of six would load up into our sedan and drive the winding road of Mulholland Drive for what seemed like hours of sisterly squabbles and some carsickness to reach the serenity of Grandpa's ranch in time for brunch. Pepper trees graced the long driveway that lead up the hill to where 'ol Prince, the St. Bernard dog, would welcome us with his massive body and wet kisses. Grandpa would greet us with his kind eyes smiling at the tradition he was creating—a family gathering with a steady diet of great memories and delicious food.

I too had a ritual, after succeeding in stuffing myself with the usual goodies of lox and bagels, coleslaw, potato pancakes with apple sauce, fresh fruit salad and the frosted poppy seed cake; I'd get bored with the adult conversation. I'd excuse myself and steal away to find and sit on my favorite deer. She was life-sized and made of bronze and was always waiting for me there on the cliff looking out over the ranch, resting on her haunches with her legs tucked under.

Once I had taken in the panorama and opened up all my senses to the familiar smells of sage, damp straw, and ranch dust, I'd emulate the same gaze she wore and drift off into the comforts of my inquiring mind. I felt immortal, without borders, and forever safe.

Reflecting like this became a regular habit for me. It was something I could do well that I truly enjoyed. Making the time to figure out things from my own perspective was a luxury that became a necessity as I moved forward in life. But back to Grandpa's ranch: By the time I had sufficiently indulged in this form of personal dessert, my food had digested enough so that I could get permission to go swimming.

The pool overlooked the expanse of land below, as it was situated on the edge of a knoll that the ranch house sat on. It had an out-sized shallow end, so us short folks could keep our heads above the water if we wanted to stand. That was one of the many things that made it clear to me that Grandpa was looking out for us. By the time I climbed out, I was completely pruned. The skin on my hands were especially white and shrivelled. I'd play like an old lady monster and scare my little brother.

The mention of going down to the stables with Grandpa to go riding was the most effective way to get us out of the pool. Glowing with pride as he walked us down the hill, Grandpa pointed out things, giving us a tour. His joy he had in his sleek racehorses in their immaculate stalls came shining through. We'd then mount an older, gentler mare who trotted around him as he called out guidance on how to stay in the saddle.

I'll never forget how honored and special I felt when Grandpa took me to the stall of a newly born prize racehorse colt that he had bred. He had named the colt, "Cass." He told me he named it after me because he knew she was a "winner!" She was the most beautiful horse I had ever seen, and I was the proudest I'd ever been.

Never one to lecture us directly, Grandpa shared his love and reverence for Nature and the Land by demonstrating the delight he got from making it his home. He loved raising thoroughbred horses, livestock, having a vegetable garden, fruit trees, and being able to collect fresh eggs from his prize chickens. He raised and butchered his own beef. He transferred to us an understanding and reverence of birth and death of his animals that he shared with us so we weren't afraid or upset by it. He knew that by living on a ranch he was showing us something of great value. And coming from the poverty he grew up in, it was also a special kind of wealth. His gratitude was real and very apparent to us. In return, he felt our appreciation, took joy in observing our reactions and the expressions on our faces as we took it all in. He had a certain quiet dignity and a presence about him that instilled in me a peace of mind and deep happiness!

In my tenth summer, I was at a boarding camp when the news came. I was called to the office and put on the phone with my dad, who told me Grandpa had passed away that morning. I went numb—the colors around me turned to black and gray. I was asked if I wanted to attend his funeral? An emphatic, "No!" came out of my mouth. My soul hurt, I was appalled by the image of Grandpa shut in a box. I would have wanted to run over, open his coffin, and somehow bring him or will him back to life. The idea of a funeral was overwhelming.

This was my first taste of profound loss, and it opened the door to many questions. What would happen to Grandpa's beloved ranch? Who would take care of the horses and honor them as he did? What about our Saturday visits? But most of all, what was I going to do without his loving smile and presence?

Change followed.

Life moved on. Yet I always had this feeling like someone or something was waiting for me. In my early 20s, while seeking a project that would encompass all that was important to me, I recalled a promise I had made to my Grandpa the last time I saw him. And so it came to pass that while raising my children, I would dedicate my life to the telling exactly who my Grandpa was and the true story of the Brothers Warner.

Getting to know more about Harry Warner, while writing this book, has been an honor and a pleasure that has allowed me to more fully understand the inner workings of and what drove the man I feel so privileged to have had in my life.

I am honored to offer you a look into Harry Warner's world—his kindness, his caring, his values and his underlying purpose to somehow make this a more understanding, better world.

Tendered with complete admiration!

– Cass Warner

Harry Warner

Who Was Harry Warner?

If Central Casting were to put out a call seeking actors to play an early twentieth century motion picture studio mogul, they would likely look for someone who could mimic the actions of a flashy, aggressive, cigar-chomping, booze guzzling, morally ambivalent chatterbox. Harry Warner, a real-life early twentieth century mogul, would never have gotten that gig.

At the height of his power he was described as being able to pass for a retired, modest-income businessman in a crowd, and apart from the occasional cigar, would have checked none of the boxes. He was a compact, strong man with a cupid bow mouth, who was considered one of the most powerful men in Hollywood.

His looks were described in the following way by *The Morning Telegraph* on April 30, 1933, when he was fifty-one-years old:

> *"He had a shrewd, owlish, quizzical face whose good nature expressed condescension towards life. Good humor was written across his features. It was not an unsophisticated kindliness, but a tolerant friendliness, which only the bitterest struggle through life can leave. He had shaggy, thick eyebrows, vivid eyes dimmed by tired eyelids, and a long upper lip with a deep ravine in the center, which ended over expressive, farcical thick lips. He had profound lines from nose to lips, which surrounded the ends of the mischievous mouth like brackets, defiant nostrils, and a chin whose tremendous strength survived a neat cleft below the life. Humor plus wise deliberateness combined gave his face a striking solidity."*

And later in the same article:

> *"History will preserve for him a special niche as the godfather of the talking screen."*

As the oldest and most responsible of the four Warner brothers, Harry, at an early age took on the paternalistic leadership of the entire family and their business endeavors. He possessed an intense work ethic and was an early riser throughout his whole life. He was said to be an unpretentious, devoted family man, home every night for dinner and content to sit at the dinner table with people whose names could seldom be found in the phone book, let alone the social register. Unlike many of his contemporaries in show business, he never sought out the company of his stars and never succumbed to the temptations of the flesh readily available to a man in his position.

Conservative in dress, he preferred blue and gray suits, but was occasionally seen sporting a cane to present a more sophisticated presence. He claimed to have no interested in athletics, but was an excellent swimmer and dancer, owned fifteen sets of golf clubs, and was a personal friend of American golfer Bobby Jones.

As the man who headed the studio that brought voices and music to the movies, it should come as no surprise that he was a big fan of the opera even though he was known to fall asleep during the performance. Breeding thoroughbred horses gave him great pleasurable. He loved going to the races, and helped found Hollywood Park Racetrack in 1938. An accomplished rider, he only gave it up after being thrown by a horse and breaking his leg.

He was a man of distinct likes and dislikes and would speak his mind freely. He trusted implicitly, but only those within his inner circle, and was often described by business rivals as both very shrewd and very proud. Harry played the role of strategic general for the family business and was often the taskmaster both in the family and in the company. In the early days, before long-term success was assured, he demanded of himself and his brothers to lead frugal lives. He loved that he and his brothers were great dreamers, but was constantly concerned about how to cover the costs of running the studio and producing the movies they did.

One aspect of his personality that fit the mold of the movie producer, he was often preoccupied with his own thoughts. His primary interest in life was making sure the movies helped make "Educated, Entertained and Enlightened" audiences with their messages. (This was the brothers' original motto for their studio.)

Harry abhorred all forms of human prejudice and persecution. As Fortune Magazine wrote in its December 1937 issue, "Harry Warner's hand is raised against the injustices he has felt and hopes others will not have." As an immigrant who grew up seeing poverty and oppression first-hand, he developed an almost mythical belief in American patriotism and was the first mogul to lash out against the coming of the Nazis in Germany.

With little or no formal education, Harry Warner became a financial wizard who was able to more than hold-his-own with the fancy financiers of Wall Street. His brother Jack said, "Without my brother Harry's financial wizardry we would not have had the cash to run the company or make the movies. He had the toughness of a brothel madam, and the buzzing persistence of a mosquito on a hot night. He could sell bathing suits to Eskimos."

While conservative in his personal lifestyle, he was willing to take huge risks to create the company he wanted; often gambling every cent on the next project. Although untrained, Harry was known as a great orator and debater, and a master of the art of cross-examination. He was also a sharp arbitrator, known on the lot as "the court of appeals" for his ability to solve disputes between actors, producers, directors, writers, idea men, salesmen, exhibitors, and often over-skeptical attorneys.

There were no film schools at the time, nonetheless, Harry developed a keen sense of story and talent. He was famous for finding the proverbial orchid in the cabbage patch or or discovering talented young players and turning them into stars with the proper build-up. But he was careful not to coddle his creations, never letting the temperamental outbreaks of his stars upset ongoing productions or his mental equilibrium.

A creative problem solver, Harry enjoyed the challenge of figuring out solutions to problems, whether on the set, or in the lives of his employees and family. He often gave advice to his underlings on the best remedies for a head cold, how to reduce interest rates on a mortgage, where to buy the best insurance policies, etc. He had several employees on the studio lot who would report to him on who was going through tough times, as he liked to anonymously donate money to help. Due to his altruism, Harry Warner was referred to as, "The man who brought charity to Hollywood".

The Warner Family in 1890.
Back row, from left to right: Albert, Harry, Ben, Pearl, and Anna.
Front row, from left to right: Sam, Fannie, and Rose.

The Beginning

Our story begins with Benjamin Wonsal, anglicized to Ben Warner, He was born on July 10th 1857 in Tsarist Russia in a Pale of Settlement (a region where Jews were allowed to reside permanently, whereas beyond those territories, Jewish residency was mostly forbidden) in a shtetl or small village called Karnosielec in Maków County on the river Orzyc in east-central Poland, which is 90 km north of Warsaw. (In the 1880's this area was part of the Russian Empire.)

On September 26, 1876 at age 19, Ben married eighteen-year-old Pearl Leah Eichelbaum, who was born and raised in the same shtetl. Their first daughter, Cecilia, arrived about a year later; then Anna, a second daughter came into the family a year after that.

In 1881, at the age of four, Cecilia passed away which was not uncommon for children in the village. Later that year on December 12 1881, to their delight, their firstborn son, Hirsz Mojzesz Wonsal—Americanized to Harry Morris Warner.

Harry's younger brother Jack described the village of Karnosielec in his book *My First Hundred Years in Hollywood*:

"Both my parents were born in the village of Karnosielec, near the German border. The only man I ever knew who could pronounce it was comedian Harry Einstein, and he only did it accidentally when he was clearing his throat before going on the radio one day.

Never having been to Karnosielec, let alone knowing how to spell it, I have had to rely on second-hand reports from my father—reports which while not entirely secretive, could not be called informative or enthusiastic.

The streets there had been gouged out of the earth, and when horsemen thundered across the rutted dirt the dust puffed up over the town and hung like a brown shroud. Most of the homes were roofed with clay and straw, and those citizens who could afford animals kept them inside the house. Life in Karnosielec, it seems was a sort of year-round country fair—with cows, goats, and pigs wandering in and out of houses as they pleased...

As in villages anywhere, there was a dark, smoky tavern where the town elders gathered to puff their clay pipes and sip warm beer as they stirred up the ashes of the past and offered the wisdom of their age to the younger men.

Perhaps there is a kind of serenity and philosophy distilled from the bitter seeds of hunger and poverty and persecution. In Karnosielec there was not much else. My father, like his father before him, was barred by the Russians from going to school because he was a Jew. So the ghetto families in the village had to steal their knowledge. Like conspirators in crime, they herded their children into the largest stable available, and there the rabbi taught them the lore of their religion and race."

Around this time, the Cossack soldiers would raid and do destruction to the Jewish town or shtetl, rape the women, round up the able men and took them to work camps. It was becoming more and more dangerous."

Jack continues:

"My father recalled that there was always a lookout posted in a loft where he could cry alarm at the approach of the village police. The secret classes ended at once. And the children, long trained in the arts of escape, crawled through a crude earth and rock tunnel into the Christian cemetery. Because tradition made it a sacred little island where the law dared not trespass, the Jewish children huddled in a cave beneath the gravestones and were safe...

One day after spending countless hours at the cobbler's bench, Ben met another mender named Waleski, who was considered the community nitwit. He told my father that he had had enough of the Cossacks and the hunger, and pants pockets that never held more than a zloty or two. He said he was to work his way to America on a cattle boat and never come back—a goal which suggested that perhaps he was not such a dope after all."

In early 1887, long after the conversation with the "village idiot" had been forgotten, Ben received a wrinkled and worn letter from Waleski, who had made it to America. The letter, which a friend helped the illiterate Ben to read said, "Come to Baltimore... riches... earn $2 a day... the streets run with gold. Everyone in America wears shoes!" There was a return address on the envelope. Ben folded it and put it in a special place.

In 1888, a decision was made: 31-year-old, Jewish cobbler known as Ben Wonsal left the small village of Karnosielec. He kissed his wife and children, checked that the family heirloom—a pocket watch was safely sewn in a pocket in his pants, and he set out to Hamburg, Germany, where he and two of his wife's brothers bought steerage tickets on an English vessel called *Chester*. In Liverpool, England, they bought the cheapest tickets to America on the British steamship *S.S. Polynesian*. Ben declared his occupation as a shoemaker. The ship departed for America on January 16, 1888. The ship made stops in Halifax, Nova Scotia, and in Londonderry, New Hampshire, before arriving in Castle Garden[1], New York's immigration station on February 3, 1888. Ben told the immigration official that his last name was "Wonsal." After several attempts to understand the pronunciation, the immigration officer wrote down "Warner."

Ben made his way to Baltimore, where to his sorrow he found the streets were not paved with gold nor did he find Waleski at the address that was on the envelope Ben had carefully brought with him.

A year and a half later, in October 1889, 31-year-old, Pere Urnal also known as Pearl Warner, was listed as a "male peddler" when she boarded the steamship to join her husband, Ben. (I've often wondered how she got the cash from Ben to buy the tickets?) Somehow, she managed to get not only herself from her little village to Bremen, Germany and then to Castle Gardens, New York, but also nine-year-old Rivka, anglicized to Anna; eight-year-old Hirsch whose name became Harry when he came to America; five-year-old, Abraham, known as Albert or Abe and; four-year-old Schmul or Sam; as well as three-year-old Henry. They bought steerage tickets and boarded the steamship *Hermann*. (Steerage was the cheapest or lowest possible category of travel. Those in steerage usually survived on salted and preserved meat, oatmeal and dried potatoes. Three slept on a 6-foot-square berth—less room than in a coffin. The berths were stacked three high in the bottom of the ship where cargo is stored.) It took five to seven weeks to cross the Atlantic. Pearl, and the five children arrived in the winter of 1889 to Castle Garden. Harry was instructed to take off his shirt so it could be burned as he arrived with a bad case of lice. He would later say that he "came to America without a shirt on my back!"

The family settled in Baltimore, Maryland, which was about three hours from where they landed. Their father Ben had set up a shoe shop

---

1   Castle Garden was also known as Fort Clinton—a circular sandstone fort at the southern end of Manhattan just across the bay from Ellis Island in New York. It was the first American immigration processing station, predating Ellis Island. The Statue of Liberty was finished being assembled in 1886, so it was seen by those arriving in New York. Ellis Island opened in 1892.

near the Central Square. It was the first of its kind as his sign read "Shoes Repaired While You Wait."

Being enterprising was a skill all the boys learned early on as the family was growing by a child a year, even though three of the twelve didn't live past four years of age.

In 1891, Ben had heard from a friend that a new railroad was being built in Virginia. He immediately thought he could sell the workers supplies like pots, pans, and food items. He bought a horse and wagon, packed it full of goods and headed to Virginia. Harry, at ten years old, was left to be the head of the household and run the Baltimore family business.

While on the road, Ben met a man who told him there was good money to be made trading supplies to Canadian trappers for fur. They became partners. Ben announced to Pearl that they were moving to Canada. For the next two years, they lived like nomads from trading post to trading post bartering supplies for pelts. Ben would unload furs and ship them to Montreal, confident that his fortune was growing. When Ben arrived at the warehouse where he was told by his partner the furs were stored, he discovered his partner was gone as were the furs.

Without a source of money, the family moved back to Baltimore. Thirteen-year-old Harry worked with Ben cobbling shoes. The other boys sold newspapers, and had a shoe shine stand that they fought for the right to set up on a busy corner in Baltimore. It was agreed that they would bring home $2 every night from their labors, so they could put this money in the family pot. For example, Sam at age 12 was running a portable gambling hall in a street fair. The customer put a nickel down and spun an arrow. He could not win less than one cigar for the nickel and he might win any number up to seven. The percentage was good for the enterprising Sam as he only paid one cent apiece for the cigars. At the age of thirteen, he was barking for an egg-dodger, and at fourteen a manager for an intemperate snake-eater. He had a brief career as a boxer, and became a locomotive fireman on the Erie.

Dapper Harry

In 1896, at age 15, Harry heard about thousands of Poles working in steel mills in Youngstown, Ohio. It sounded like an opportunity for him to repair a lot of shoes. He rented a small vacant store and set himself up for business. He stood in the store's window, hammer in hand, mouth full of nails and repaired shoes. He was an instant sidewalk attraction, and became so overwhelmed with business that he wrote his father urging him to join him.

Ben loaded up their wagon, and moved the whole Warner family to Smoky Hollow, which was on the northside of Youngstown, Ohio. (It was called "Smoky Hollow" because the steel mills weren't far away, and the smoke and pollution got trapped in the "Hollow.") Harry encouraged Ben to also open a grocery store that sold and delivered meat.

In 1899, the bicycle craze was sweeping Youngstown. Eighteen-year-old Harry and fourteen-year-old Abe went into a bicycle shop to buy two bikes. The cost was $30 a bike, a tidy sum for the day, and not something the brothers had. Harry offered to pay cash for one, and pay off the other in thirty days, but the owner refused to give credit. Harry left the shop and turned to Albert and said he had just decided to get into the bicycle business. They made good money repairing and selling bikes as well as renting them for 15 cents an hour. They, also, had a bowling alley which gave them an insight into the drawing power of amusements.

Young Sam Warner

Meanwhile, Sam took a job in an amusement park where he learned to use a kinetoscope projector, which was recently invented. There was a large tent with a passenger train car inside it, where the audience sat. The projector was situated on the top of the car of the train. The audience inside saw images projected on the sides of the tent that made them feel like they were traveling on the train as the train was rocked back and forth as if it was moving and they were shown the Grand Canyon out their window.

In 1903, Sam invited Harry to go to a nickelodeon in Pittsburgh, Pennsylvania, where Harry was working in a clothing store. They saw a one-reel Western, "The Great Train Robbery." They watched it three times, before they were asked to leave. Standing outside they stood and watched the nickels being put on the plate by the enthusiastic audiences, they looked at each other, shook hands and said, "We're in the business."

The dream was born! Sam found a second-hand projector that was for sale. The family pooled their money and they pawned old Bob, the horse that pulled their meat delivery wagon and Ben's prize possession—the family heirloom watch.

Sam located empty store fronts in towns in Ohio to hang a sheet and show "The Great Train Robbery" until an arrangement to use a theatre in the booming steel mill town of Newcastle, Pennsylvania happened in 1907. Embarrassed by a scarcity of chairs, they worked out a deal with the undertaker next door to use their chairs. It was not unusual for a funeral to wait while patrons of the theater watched the movie or for patrons to stand to watch the movie when a funeral was taking place. Sister Rose played the rented piano, and Jack sang the songs, in his teenage voice that would sometimes crack, while the lyrics were shown on the screen. This assisted in chasing people out of the theater so the next crowd could come in. Women, in those days, would not attend such amusement places as they were unlit. Harry came up with the bright idea to put in modest oil lights along the sides of the interior which resulted in feminine patronage becoming normal.

Getting audiences to attend was no problem, but acquiring good films was. In spring of 1907, the brothers started a distribution exchange in Pittsburgh called "The Duquesne Amusement & Supply Co." Sam and Abe went to New York City and bought films instead of renting them. They bought 3 trunks of films for $500, and then they rented them out and were making about $2,500 a week, an impressive sum for those days. At the time, there were about 7 or 8 companies producing films keeping them supplied.

Harry along with several other theatre operators around New Castle, decided to form an exchange. From then on, the people distributing film were referred to as "The Exchange." They'd buy a film from the movie producer and rent it to the individual theatre owners. Harry had realized, the big money was not in showing films but in renting them out.

They were successful until 1908, when Thomas Edison established his "Trust"—the Motion Pictures Patent Co.—to force exhibitors to pay him for the use of his projector. No film could be shown or produced in the U.S. without a Patent Co. license. The Trust forced the Warners to sell their exchange or face ruin. Edison and company would also send thugs to physically intimidate them. Given no option, they sold. "If you break us, you'll break yourselves," Harry Warner told the head of the General Film Company, an organization formed by the Motion Picture Patents Company in an attempt to monopolize distribution. This was prophetic. The Warners and other independents began making their own pictures, and in five years the General Film Company had failed.

When Carl Laemmle took a stand against the Edison gang by forming the Independent Motion Picture Co. and setting up exchanges in major cities, Harry, decided to move into production and use Laemmle's organization for distribution.

The Warner's first picture was *The Covered Wagon* with only one wagon. They called it *The Peril Of the Plains*. They made several other successful four and five-reelers, but in their haste to expand, went outside of the family to take in partners. The new partners knew copartnership law. The Warners did not. Their company was doing beautifully, but the four brothers had signed away everything but the debts. They not only sold their homes but called in the old-clothes man to sell their clothes. After discharging their own obligations, they raised eighteen thousand dollars to pay off the losses of friends who had invested in the wrong issue of securities.

When their affairs were wound up, the four Warners had one dollar and sixty-five cents between them. They soon found a backer, however, and started to distribute foreign-made pictures, making money with the French film *Redemption*, but losing everything in 1917 in a futile effort to educate the public to appreciate *The Glass Coffin*.

Then they began to look about for a new start. Passing a bookstore window, Sam pointed out a picture of a fly with the face of Ambassador James W. Gerard in a web surrounded by spiders with the faces of the Kaiser. It was an advertisement for Gerard's book, *My Four Years in Germany*. Harry contacted the Ambassador and persuaded him that taking their offer of twenty percent of the profits in return for the film rights was what he should do.

A backer put up forty thousand dollars, while Sam and Jack went to Hollywood and built a studio and print laboratory with their own hands, and Albert Warner began to sell the picture in advance as "the greatest ever made."

First exhibited while World War I was still ongoing, *My Four Years in Germany* was a sensation, grossing eight hundred thousand dollars.

In Harry's Own Words

The following excerpts are taken from writings and speeches made by Harry Warner, or articles written about him on a variety of topics in chronological order. (In a few cases, these writings have been edited for brevity and clarity.)

All the Brothers Were Valiant: Harry and Sam, Abe and Jack Have Never Repudiated Their Own Declaration of Independence

DOROTHY DONNELL

In 1909 the brothers immigrated to New York with the high idea of becoming producers themselves. They announced themselves as "Warner Features," the first independent motion picture company, and began to buy up and distribute an odd medley of pictures. They have remained independents ever since.

The Warner Features flourished, as film companies went in those days. Sam at 26 years old, and Jack at 18 years old came to California two years later to make a picture, ***Are Passions Inherited?*** with Dot Farley as the star. Such gems of art as these did not make the four brothers rich, but they attracted after a while the attention of the General Film Corporation. They noticed that none of the Warners wore expensive tailoring or sported diamonds in their ties. It noticed the steady gaze of Harry Warner, the strength of Albert's profile, the grim jaw of Sam, the unquenchable and sunny smile of Jack. It noticed that in whatever these four brothers did they thought spoke and acted as one.

Whereupon Thomas Edison's company, the General Film Corporation, cannily put the Warner Features out of business, and then generously offered to refinance them as part of their organization.

"What about it boys?" asked Harry, the eldest. "Do we stay on our own, or do we work for them?"

"We stay independent," said Sam, Abe, Harry and Jack with one voice. The result was that they found themselves walking down Broadway smoking cigars and confidently discussing buying a best seller and making a feature motion picture, ***My Four Years in Germany*** without a cent in the world.

Sam Warner had this to say, "I had nerve and plenty of it to go after anything that I thought we needed, and I figured we needed a chance to make a picture of the Ambassador Gerard story more than we needed anything else in the world. So, I telegraphed Mr. Gerard that we were the largest motion picture company in the United States. I knew he had been in Germany for four years and I figured he couldn't check up on us. I got an answer to my wire which caused me to wire Harry to go to see him at once and Harry did and closed the deal. Mr. Gerard agreed to take 20 per cent of the profits for the rights to the story. Then we had the rights and no money. Finally, we found a backer, made the picture, and that picture put us on our feet."

In 1918, *My Four Years in Germany* was timed exactly right for success. With the proceeds, the brothers moved to Hollywood. They bought a vacant lot with a wooden shed upon it, proudly thereafter referred to as "the studio." Sam and Jack in between intervals of making comedies with Monty Banks and Al St. John, persuaded his stars to help him lay a plank across the stretch of mud to walk on what was referred to grandly as "the lot."

For three years the Warner Brothers produced lurid serials, animal pictures and short comedies in these humble quarters without attracting the envious attention of the Hollywood gods.

Then they flung their first display of strength into the faces of the big fellows in Hollywood. They announced a series of "**Seven Classics of the Screen**." It was the first time that any movie producer had considered paying large sums for the picture rights of popular novels. "They'll never get their money back. They're crazy."

A huge truck, painted with immense books taller than a man with titles of the seven best sellers emblazoned on their spine crossed the continent from New York to Hollywood. The Warner Brothers found bigger theaters opening their doors to show their products.

The Warners first major production premiered in New York on May 21, 1918. The film netted $130,000 in profits.

Sam and Jack returned to Los Angeles and set up the first studio near downtown. When they needed more space, they purchased a 10-acre lot in Hollywood for $25,000 with nothing down and built a large studio with a mammoth stage on the lot. Warner Bros. West Coast Studios was born.

The brothers began to create their signature-type, socially conscious films with:

Parted Curtains (1920)

This was the embryo of future gangster films. A convict is released from jail and cannot find a job so he resorts to desperation and steals from a painter, who in turn shows compassion and sets about to rehabilitate the convict.

Ashamed of Parents (1921)

A story about a shoemaker, whose attempts to make a decent living for his family is paralleled by his struggle to send his son to college.

Why Girls Leave Home (1921)

Focuses on the corrupting effects of big city life on small town, and innocent people.

School Days (1921)

A youngster's small-town upbringing leaves him unprepared for the sophistication of New York's elite society, so he briefly turns to the underworld of crime, and ultimately finds spiritual redemption and returns to his small town.

Robin Hood (1922)

A nobleman becomes the vigilante Robin Hood who protects the oppressed English people from the tyrannical Prince John. It stands as one of the earliest anti-fascist films on record.

The Gold Diggers (1923)

The life of two sisters who enter the world of showgirls. One risks everything to ensure her sister's happiness.

The Age of Innocence (1924)

A member of a straight-laced family finds himself in the middle of a scandal when he has an affair with a Polish countess, who when she discovers that her lover's wife is pregnant, breaks off the affair and moves back to Poland.

There were two assets Sam and Jack Warner acquired in 1923 that helped the studio blossom. The wildly successful **Rin Tin Tin** movies. (Rin Tin Tin was fed steaks and nicknamed "The Mortgage Lifter") and Darryl F. Zanuck, a prodigious screenwriter, creating more than 15 scripts in a year.

"It is a natural thing for a person to feel discouraged, especially after he has worked hard and thought right without realizing any tangible results. That's just the time to buck up and fight a little harder." –Harry Warner

Warner Brothers Plan $10,000,000 in Transcontinental Theatre Chain

Moving Picture World
SEPTEMBER 20, 1924

Independent producers like Warner Bros. are suffering because of the exhibitor's inability to consider the independent product purely on its own merits due to the sales methods and monopolies of the big distributors and studios. Harry Warner is traveling to the East Coast with the goal of choosing sites to build a chain of new theaters to overcome the problems of distribution.

Harry Warner: "It has never been our wish – or a part of our plan – to engage in the exhibition end of the motion picture business. Today we would be perfectly satisfied to go on producing photoplays only if the exhibiting trade at large were in a position to give us what we consider a halfway run for our money. We have been making a line of photoplays, which are worthy of exhibition in the best theatres in the country and we think many of them a lot better, and more to the public's taste, than many others which are being given preferred booking. Our determination to build theatres wherever we find it necessary in order to get this 'halfway' run for our money is one that has been forced upon us by the same "Trust" practices which are harassing independent exhibitors throughout the country to death. For this reason, we feel that we are in no sense deviating from our original policy, which was to support the weaker members of the industry at large. We are taking off our coats to do battle – but in no sense can the exhibition as a class to be considered our adversaries. We're going to fight the combinations which we are satisfied are out to ruin the industry for everyone but themselves. And in many instances our operation in the exhibiting end of the business will bring to the independent exhibitor the strength he needs to stave off destruction."

"A new era in motion picture presentation has arrived. It will thrill and startle the world. The marvelous Vitaphone process will revolutionize the industry. It will make it possible for small town theatres to have the same musical accompaniment as that enjoyed in the biggest theatres the world over." –Harry Warner

Sam Warner decided to go into radio when other studios thought radio was a competing plague. He started KFWB in Los Angeles. It was majorly fortuitous because the engineers who built it for them, a man who worked for Western Electric, told Sam about a fantastic innovation he had seen at Bell Labs— sound movies.

Kings of the Talkies

The New Yorker
DECEMBER 22, 1928

The men who murdered the silent drama are the four Warner Brothers: Harry, Albert, Jack, and the late Sam Warner. History will hold them equally guilty.

They were not the first to make the pictures talk. Years before, Thomas Edison, Lee de Forest, and others had caused the screen to soliloquize in empty houses, but the Warners were the first to make the public listen.

The modern talking-picture mechanism was developed in the laboratories of the American Telephone and Telegraph Company in 1925. The telephone engineers saw the motion picture industry revolutionized overnight... The headliner at that premiere of the modern talkie was a full-length talking portrait of a gentleman with an impediment in his speech. Immediately after the performance the biggest man in the movies left without making any comment and was never heard from again.

That was in February 1925. In March another man was the biggest man in the industry. The apparatus was tuned up again and the new biggest man was invited to see and hear it. He said, "Gentlemen, this is horrible."

The show was then strengthened by a comic act, written and staged by two telephone engineers and a physicist, but the April and May crop of biggest men in the motion picture industry were still unimpressed. By this time every big concern except Warners had decided that the public would never like talkies.

The Warners—and this is no idle figure of speech—bet their shirts they would make the public like talkies and mortgaged everything down to their personal belongings to launch the Vitaphone. The heads of the other big companies had made fortunes gambling against fickleness of the public, but they did not want to risk their winnings. "Stabilize" and "standardize" were their watchwords, and they hated the thought of experiments and innovations. They had everything to lose by a revolution in the industry; the Warners had everything to gain.

Harry discusses taking on The Big Three exhibitioners (Famous Players, First National, and Loews) who he believes are trying to gain a monopoly on all the theaters in the country and in the process wiping out the independent producers and theater owners. He claimed that they (The Big Three) were spending too much time trying to buy theaters rather than focusing on improving their product. To fight their attacks head-on, Warner Bros. announced they were going to build a $1,000,000 theater that would be the most prestigious in the country.

Warner Brothers Join Attack on Film Trust

Los Angeles Times
MAY 14, 1925

In Harry Warner's words, "We wish we did not have to build theaters and could devote our efforts to the production of high-class pictures. We believe that the original theater owners in a community should reap the benefits of the development in the industry. It is a Napoleonic desire for more and more power that is behind the movement for monopoly. Personally, I believe in letting the little fellow live. I can make enough money out of pictures to satisfy me."

Warner Bros. was the studio that broke the sound barrier in film. The following documents describe their step-by-step movements into sound starting with their acquisition of Vitagraph Pictures and their development of the Vitaphone sound process, the decision to add music and effects to **Don Juan***, followed by their production of the film,* **The Jazz Singer***, when audiences everywhere first heard an actor's voice on screen.*

Talking pictures or "Talkies" had a horrible reputation at the time. The actors' mouths weren't synchronized with the words coming out of their mouths. The audience was so frustrated that they'd throw tomatoes at the screen.

At one time, (the) Warners were distributing their pictures by a system of independent agents who got big percentages from their territories. Most of them had contracts expiring in September 1925. The agents got together and believed they had Warner Bros. at their mercy for new, more favorable contracts.

Here again, Harry Warner beat the financial wolves at their own game. There was little doubt that various financial interests, probably egged on by rival producers, had put the agents up to their tricks. Harry made up his mind to buy Vitagraph, which would give him another means of distributing his pictures as well as provide greater production facilities. All he needed was a few million dollars.

Vitagraph had its own exchanges in 30 cities of the U.S. and an elaborate foreign system. Vitagraph was slipping. Harry decided this was their big chance. To shorten a long story of painful negotiations, Warners bought Vitagraph for $800,000 besides taking over their debts of $980,000. The papers were drawn up in longhand and Harry wrote a check for $100,000.

The next day, Harry told the bankers about it. When asked what it involved, Harry replied, "1.5 million dollars." They told him he'd better get more capital for a cushion. The result of this discussion was a check for $4,000,000. Bankers were beginning to believe in the Warners!

Harry made an unexpected find in Vitagraph. He not only put the deal through but was better off than he had ever expected to be by a hefty million dollars.

Most of Harry Warner's time was being spent dickering with loan sharks, sometimes paying as much as 40 percent for the money until Waddill Catchings, a financier of extraordinary abilities, came along in December 1924.

Catchings said, "It was not their work in pictures so much as their extremely simple private lives that gave me confidence in them." He was the one real source of money they used to buy Vitagraph, which enabled them to free themselves from the franchise holders and agents.

Sam invited Harry to a demonstration of Vitagraph sound at the Bell Laboratory. It was of an orchestra on the screen with its music swinging out into space that gave Harry a bright idea.

Here is what Harry wrote to his brother when he got back to his office:

"Sam, I wouldn't be so foolish as to try and make talking pictures. That's what everybody else has done and lost. No, we'll do better than that we can use this thing for other purposes. We can use it for musical accompaniment for our pictures. We can film and record vaudeville acts and make up programs for houses that can't afford the real thing or can't get the big-time acts. Think of what it would mean to a small independent theater owner to buy his own orchestra with pictures."

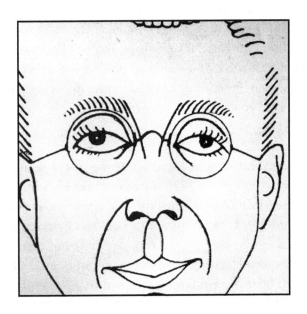

Harry Warner

Working and Thinking

Brass Tacks
JULY 10, 1926

"It is no secret. The two big essentials for success are right thinking and hard work. The man that thinks right and works hard can't help but succeed. Thinking and working are an unbeatable combination.

Now there comes a time in every person's life when he gets discouraged. It is a natural thing for a person to feel discouraged, especially after he has worked hard and thought right without realizing any tangible results. That's just the time to buck up and fight a little harder. Don't let discouragement lick you. Success is just around the corner.

Exhibitors all over the country have made a fortune with our pictures. We are giving them the right product: real box-office entertainment, and with good product an exhibitor can always cash in. Incidentally, there isn't another company in the business that is offering them pictures such as we are offering right now.

One's efforts will make it easier later. You will have paved, by your efforts, the road to success for the future product while the other fellows are off on vacation. Push a little harder, don't get discouraged work hard, think right, keep going. You can't go wrong!"

"As for the educational possibilities of the instrument, I believe that not even the surface has yet been scratched, and that it will only be a question of time until most of the schools and colleges in the country will make use of it. Lectures by the greatest of all professors may now go the rounds instead of being merely presented in one classroom. Students will not have to travel far and wide to hear certain famous learned men." – Harry Warner

The Future of Vitaphone

Harry M. Warner
Variety
JULY 24, 1926

"Vitaphone will thrill the world for it will give to millions of people in the most remote localities the thrill that only music, the universal language, can engender. As the motion picture has contributed to the peace of the world by giving to all peoples a greater and more truthful understanding of each other, so this new invention will contribute to the world's happiness by carrying to all men in all countries the beauty and contentment, the peace and enjoyment that only the compositions rendered by the supreme artists of modern times can give. Shakespeare in his wisdom said, 'The man that hath no music in himself, now is not moved by concord of sweet sounds, is fit for treasons, stratagems and spoils. Let no such man be trusted.' Shakespeare knew humanity as few men have.

Fortunately for mankind, I believe that there are not very many such unfortunates in the world. In some, because of environment, perhaps, the musical instinct is dormant. Vitaphone will awaken it, and so contribute to the joy of living.

In conclusion, let me quote Professor Pupin of Colombia University. He says in effect: 'What wouldn't I give if today could see and hear Abraham Lincoln deliver his Gettysburg Address?' Posterity, through Vitaphone, will be able to see and hear the great ones of the present and future generations. Once more I wish to utter the prophecy, Vitaphone will thrill the world."

Deliver the Message to the Exhibitors Around the World

Brass Tacks
JULY 24, 1926

Picture This!!

The greatest artists of the operatic and musical field can be heard in the smallest of theatres as well as the largest. Millions of people will be educated to a finer appreciation of the best music that has ever been written by the foremost composers.

Imagine! The wonderful New York Philharmonic Orchestra – 107 pieces in a small town!! The synchronization of music and motion picture is an established fact, and on August 6th the great invention will be heard by the public at a deluxe world's premiere presentation in conjunction with the film *Don Juan*, one of the biggest road show attractions of the year.

Spread the message and deliver it to the exhibitors of the world!!

Explanation of New Device that Gave Hollywood Kick

Variety "Don Juan"—Vitaphone Special
AUGUST 5, 1926

Hollywood was given the thrill and surprise of its electrically lighted life tonight, when the Vitaphone was heard for the first time publicly on the Pacific coast at Grauman's Egyptian Theatre in conjunction with the showing of "**Don Juan**," the widely heralded photoplay starring John Barrymore.

"How do they do it?" was a question heard on all sides, after the audience had awakened to the fact that the entrancing symphony music that accompanied the film was actually being reproduced and was not being played from behind the screen by a cleverly hidden orchestra.

All the echoes that had been coming from the Manhattan Opera House in New York, which the Vitaphone Corporation had converted into a huge studio and laboratory, at once assumed tangible form. First-nighters became conscious that they were listening to a revolutionary instrument, and that would be far-reaching in its effects...

Vitaphone is absolutely nothing like any other invention. The principles underlying the instrument are different entirely from other attempts that have been made at the reproduction of sound in conjunction with motion pictures. In essence, Vitaphone embodies the combination of several recent scientific developments. These are an electrical system of registering sound waves that have been registered.

The first step in registration is accomplished by means of a high-quality microphone of an improved type, complemented by an electrical amplifying apparatus and sound registering mechanism. Registration may be carried on at a considerable distance from the source of the sound. This is quite an important feature, as it enables the soloists or actors to group themselves naturally in any scene and does away with crowding before a microphone.

The second step in the process depends upon a device that reproduces the sound waves that have been registered. Electrical currents from this device pass into an amplifier and operate a powerful loud speaker. This speaker is of a type that eliminates any mechanical sound and is capable of creating sufficient volume to fill any size auditorium.

The third step is to link up the reproducer so the music will be made audible to those seated in a theatre. An adaption of the public address system makes it possible to pick up the registered sound waves, amplifying them, and by means of properly located loud speaking telephones transform the waves, or vibrations into sound. The volume is so regulated as to create the illusion that actors, whose pictures appear on the screen, are in reality speaking or singing or playing, as the case may be. For musical programs, a specially constructed loud speaking telephone insures correct volume and naturalness.

Synchronization—that is, the perfect dovetailing of motion picture and sound, whether an address or a solo by an artist with full orchestral accompaniment—is affected as follows. Microphones placed at strategic points picked up each note of voice and instrument, and these were transmitted to the laboratory for registration. An idea of the complexity of this part of the process may be had when it is pointed out that the switchboard through which the sounds are transmitted for registration is more intricate in design than that of the largest radio broadcast station.

So sensitive is the registration apparatus, that the master camera that controls it had to be enclosed in a soundproof box, to prevent its "clickety-click" from being passed into the laboratory with the sounds it was desired to reproduce. A musician who is also an electrical engineer sits at the switchboard, with a marked score of the music in front of him and controls the volume according to a predetermined plan.

When it became necessary to reproduce the pictures and music that had been registered, another apparatus was employed. This is less complicated than the mechanism used in the reproduction process. The reproducing apparatus transmits the sound waves over electric wires to sounding boards placed above and below the screen, and in the orchestra pit. The net effect is the voice coming from the singer and the instruments being heard in their proper places in the orchestra pit.

The Vitaphone comes to the public as the result of years of research in the Western Electric Company and the Bell Telephone laboratories, supplemented by the efforts of Walter J. Rich and the Warner brothers...

An important use of the Vitaphone will be in providing musical programs for motion pictures that have already been filmed. This is accomplished by projecting the picture in the usual way and registering the music, previously cued, in synchronization with the film. Any picture which has ever been produced can be orchestrated and synchronized. The sound synchronization is not dependent on recording at the time of the exposure of the film.

The Vitaphone apparatus by means of which the combination of motion pictures and sound is reproduced in the theatre is no more complicated from the standpoint of operation, than an ordinary motion picture projector. No special skill or technical knowledge is required of the operator. If the film breaks, there is not interference with the accuracy of synchronization. The sound registration is controlled by the film itself.

To develop the Vitaphone, and to make the synchronization of music available to motion picture producers throughout the world, and to distribute it among theatre owners, there has been formed the Vitaphone Corporation. The board of directors of this corporation includes Walter J. Rich, president; Samuel L. Warner, first vice-president; Eugene C.C. Rich, second vice-president; Albert Warner, treasurer, and Waddill Catchings.

New Era in Motion Pictures, Says Hays of Vitaphone: Motion Picture Czar, First Man to Address Public Through New Device Welcomes Synchronized Music as Big Advance in Industry Sees Great Possibilities

AUGUST 5, 1926
WILLIAM H. HAYS
Variety

Declaring that the Vitaphone marked a new era in music and motion pictures, Will H. Hays, president of the Motion Picture Producers and Distributors Association, welcomed the instrument to the industry at a premiere of John Barrymore in **Don Juan** at the Warner Theater last night. Mr. Hays spoke through the Vitaphone and his voice registered as clearly as though he were present in person.

It was the only and historic first demonstration of the synchronization of the speaking voice during the evening, the rest of the program consisting of vocalists and instrumentalists. Mr. Hays said:

"My friends. No story ever written for the screen is as dramatic as the story of the screen itself. Tonight, we write another chapter in this story. For, indeed, have we advanced from that few seconds of shadow of a serpentine dancer thirty years ago when the motion picture was born—to this public demonstration of the Vitaphone synchronizing the reproduction of sound with the reproduction of action.

The future of motion pictures is as far flung as all the tomorrows, rendering greater and still greater service as the chief amusement of the majority of all our people and the sole amusement of millions and millions, exercising an immeasurable influence as a living, breathing thing on the ideas and ideals, the customs and the costumes, the hopes and ambitions of countless men, women, and children.

In the presentation of these pictures, music plays an invaluable part. The motion picture is a most potent factor in the development of a national appreciation of good music. That service will now be extended as the Vitaphone shall carry symphony orchestrations to the town halls and the hamlets.

It has been said that the art of vocalist and instrumentalist is ephemeral, and that he creates only for the moment. Now, neither the artist nor his art will ever wholly die.

Long experimentation and research by the Western Electric Company and the Bell Telephone Laboratories, supplemented by the efforts of Warner Brothers and Walter J. Rich, have made this great new instrument possible, and to them and to all who have contributed to this achievement I offer my congratulations and best wishes.

To the Warner Brothers, to whom is due credit for this, the beginning of a new era in music and motion pictures, I offer my felicitations and sincerest appreciation. It is an occasion with which the public and the motion picture industry are equally gratified. It is another great service, and Service is the supreme commitment of life."

Don Juan and Vitaphone CoStars at Warner's
John Barrymore's Superb Performance
Vitaphone Revelation for Novelty and Music
Don Juan Played by Greatest Actor in the World
Finest Romantic Story Ever Filmed
Vitaphone Climaxes Record of Show Business

Fred Schader and Sime Silverman
Variety
AUGUST 7, 1926

Girls get your season tickets early.

There's something at Warner's theater on Broadway the show business never has seen before. It's a perfect combination.

Every woman, married or single, young or old, is going to see John Barrymore as Don Juan in the Warner Brothers' picture of that name. Every woman is going to see it again and again and again!

That's the kind of picture **Don Juan** is. That's the sort of a romantic hero John Barrymore makes of him.

And the Vitaphone will get 'em all – men, women, and children.

This Vitaphone, attached to a moving picture as it is to **Don Juan** is the climax of picturedom. It's the pinnacle so often sought and never before reached.

A Double Hit

The Warner Brothers have a double hit, a two 10-strike, the unprecedented success of filmville.

In Vitaphone the Warners have an achievement. It's a novelty to the paying public and it's entertain-ment besides, while to the theatrical trade it's a godsend.

But girls! Here you have a motion picture that sends you away tingling, with the heroic Don Juan of your dreams, the sardonic Borgia for your hatred and the sweet Adriana for your model.

Unexcelled Price

In the Vitaphone for novelty and **Don Juan** both on the same bill at the one price of admission, is a composition unexcelled at the same scale. It's something the show business never has had, never has expected and probably will never see again in so complete and entertaining a form.

You may go home and safely say that never in the 25-year record of the picture-making business has there been a scene to equal the long and short sword duel of Don Juan with its unexpected twist to a hand-to-hand battle, nor never in any moving picture – "society" "action" "western" – or any other kind—has there been a flight by horse to compare with Don Juan escaping from the Borgias with his lady-love on the saddle beside him.

Nor do the records of pictures from their infancy to date reveal a motion picture film that carried its own musical accompaniment, as does **Don Juan** with the Vitaphone, to the score composed by William Axt.

The Players

In this Warner Brothers picture you will admit the directorial perfectness by Alan Crosland, the scenario as skeletonized by Bess Meredyth; the splendid playing by Mary Astor of Adriana (the role that places Mary Astor where she deserves to be); and the admirable performance by Estelle Taylor as Lucretia Borgia, a difficult villainous role, played up and down in looks and movement by Miss Taylor, who otherwise is known to more or less fame as the wife of Jack Dempsey.

Nor will a word of adverse criticism be heard against the casting of the entire playing forces of this super-production, from its principals to its "extras," and there were plenty of "extras" in many rough and wild scenes. While for production, the Warners can take a bow.

Beware Girls!

Let's hope that none of the girls shall reproach their beaux or their husbands concerning this Don Juan of John Barrymore's. That it's a great romantic story elegantly picturized does not mean that he whom you love best should go and do likewise.

But the girls will take the boys to see **Don Juan** and it will make better boys and better girls. For here is story of romance that is "clean" in spirit, in enfoldment, and in dress.

Do you want to hear a little commercialism with a mind full of a dashing fellow who loved at last, as did Don Juan? Then here it is: that the Warner Brothers in their presentation of **Don Juan** with the Vitaphone have an untold fortune before them. **Don Juan** the film will live forever. Your children will see it again 10 or 15 years from now, and again 25 or 30 years away your grandchildren will enjoy it, while the Vitaphone will go on and on; its scope is the universe.

Inoffensive Sex

There is this about the picture – that is, it is "sexy" in a manner inoffensive, but after all sex on the stage or screen is that which has meant a greater audience than any other theme, because God sexed his children. If He didn't want sex in this world there wouldn't have been Eve in the Garden of Eden. The Almighty saw fit to create man in His own image, and then take a rib from him and present him with a helpmate, and there will always be sex as long as the Almighty sees fit to let the world continue.

Likewise, all God's "Chillun" will delight in the picture **Don Juan** because it is life, love, and the redemption of man through a woman's love.

It matters not what woman be mother, wife or sweetheart. It does not matter how bad the man nor his reputation, if she be a real woman as God intended her to be she can take the worst philanderer, renegade, or atheist and restore his faith in womankind.

At least, if they do not write it, it is edited for them into the terms of "show business" which to you, as the public, is the medium whereby you can forget your cares, your woes, your tribulations and even your family spats, but which to them is just so much work, stock, merchandise or name it what you will.

If there is anything that is going to take you back to those kiddie days, where you can believe yourself the heroine or the hero of this particular fictionalization of history, **Don Juan** is the picture to do it.

Will H. Hay's Vitaphone speech was presented just prior to the balance of the features. He said, "For your entertainment, so great if not greater, is this newest development in the field that has been the outlet for human emotions, the inspiration for better thought, and let it be hoped, the foundation for a better life – the theatre."

Vitaphone the Theater

The Vitaphone IS the theatre. It is the theater to a greater extent that the motion picture by itself ever was. The screen at its best gave us but fleeting shadows. The titles in the earlier days of the screen history first gave us the story. Later, as the technique of the motion picture developed, there came something in the portrayal of action that conveyed the story without the necessity of the titles every few feet. But the combination of the motion picture and the attachment which is named the Vitaphone is going to bring to countless millions of people of the country and the world over the motion picture in a manner such as they have never seen it.

Broadway All Over

There is going to be a revolution in that selfsame, heretofore, referred to as "show business" as a result of the advent of the Vitaphone. It is going to give the country at large everything that Broadway, New York' State Street, Chicago, Broadway, and Los Angeles has had in the way of motion picture entertainment, and added to it is going to be an additional 100 per cent of value, for as the Vitaphone presentation of **Don Juan** was revealed at Warner's theatre last night brought to the blasé Broadway public of New York a new entertainment factor, so is the country at large going to get it. Just think of it – the greatest stars of every phase of the music and entertainment world brought to your own doorstep and handed to you just the same as they would be to a millionaire who has his box in the Diamond Horseshoe of the Metropolitan Opera House and give you without asking any more than they did for the average motion picture which was classed as a special attraction.

But to the scientists, the engineers, the picture people, and even to those lowly women who scrubbed and mopped the Manhattan Opera House in New York, where the musical and vocal portions of this Warner Bros. theatre program were worked out and developed it in their final stages, you Dear Mr. and Mrs. Public, do owe a debt of thanks, not only for yourselves, but for the generations that are to come.

Don Juan is Answer to Maiden's Prayer: John Barrymore Picture Has Everything in it that will Appeal to Women

Variety

Don Juan is a woman's picture.

The ladies will love it. It has everything they like. A fascinating, handsome, delightfully wicked hero; beautiful girls gorgeously gowned and a plot that will tickle their sensibilities.

Barrymore as Don Juan is the answer to every maiden's prayer. Every woman in the audience imagines herself his ladylove. He is fickle and inconstant, but that adds to his charm. He is unreliable and elusive, which makes him tantalizingly attractive. He is the man who loves no woman, but let's every woman love him.

Then, there are the beautiful Renaissance gowns worn by Mr. Barrymore's ten lovely ladies. Velvets, pearls, rubies, silks, and satins of every shade and hue adorn these beautiful girls, and at the premiere last night, evoked murmurs of envy and appreciation from the feminine portion of the audience.

The gorgeous furniture and tapestries of the Italian Renaissance play a big part in the production. The settings are all authentic, and with the modern craze for period furniture, will prove of unusual interest to women. Chairs, couches, rugs, hangings, and tables are all originals, and will delight the heart of the connoisseur.

Remarkable First Night Crowd Acclaims Vitaphone: Midsummer Audience of Celebrities and General Public Thrills at Introduction of New Instrument – Don Juan Called 'Great Picture'

Variety
AUGUST 6, 1926

History was made last night at the Warner Theatre when Warner Bros. and the Vitaphone Corporation introduced Vitaphone as a prelude to John Barrymore in **Don Juan**. It not only thrilled the remarkable first night audience ever assembled in a New York Theatre, but as prophesized, the echoes from that thrill will ring around the world.

True, it was a slightly incredulous audience that passed through the doors at 8:30 o'clock. So much has been talked and written about sound and pictures that many were only skeptical. But it was those who later passed out their warmest, enthusiastic praise of a new art that Will H. Hays said in his opening address, "is the beginning of a new era in music and pictures."

The unanimous verdict was that all the superlatives that have been used to exploit the Vitaphone have not been enough. Vitaphone is the greatest invention the world of music and pictures has yet known, and *Don Juan* from start to finish is a great production.

The Warner Theatre was jammed with celebrities. Society, Wall Street, the stage and screen were there en masse. Motion picture producers met directors, directors met stars, and the stars met society. All there to see and hear the Vitaphone and *Don Juan*.

Broadway from 51st to 52nd streets was jammed with curious onlookers. The fans were there to see the great movie turnout. Estelle Taylor had part of her wrap torn by the enthusiastic crowd, and it took all of husband Jack Dempsey's prize-ring prowess to pilot her safely into the theatres. Will Hays, Efrem Zimbalist, Anna Case and Henry Hadley, all Vitaphone artists, received a rousing ovation as they entered the theater.

At eight-thirty the house was seated. An expectant hush pervaded the theatre. The program started with a speech of welcome delivered by Will Hays on the Vitaphone. The audience had not expected such perfect synchronization, and the applause at the conclusion of Mr. Hays' address was deafening.

The musical program started with an overture from "Tannhauser," recorded by the New York Philharmonic Orchestra. The illusion was perfect. First, there was a long shot of the entire Philharmonic Orchestra, consisting of 107 musicians. As certain instruments were played, close-ups of the musicians rendering that particular portion of the piece were used. Then back to a medium shot, with the composer, Henry Hadley taking a bow at the conclusion, while the entire orchestra stood in acknowledgment of the enthusiastic applause.

Mischa Elman, famous violinist, appeared. He played "Humoresque" and would have been recalled if possible. Roy Smeck, in "His Pastimes" was flashed on the screen. Smeck played several jazz numbers, first on a guitar, then on a ukulele and finished with a number on the banjo.

Marion Talley, with her rendition of Caro Nome from "Rigoletto" stirred the audience to another enthusiastic burst of applause. The youthful prima donna from Kansas City made an exquisitely appealing figure. Many in the audience were hearing her for the first time.

Efrem Zimbalist on the violin and Harold Bauer on the piano played the variations from "Kruetzer Sonata" by Beethoven and were followed by Giovanni Martinelli, who sang Vesti la Giubba from "II Pagliacci," accompanied by the New York Philharmonic Orchestra. Martinelli was a riot. The house applauded, cheered and stamped its feet.

Anna Case, supported by the Cansinos and Metropolitan Opera chorus and accompanied by the Vitaphone Symphony Orchestra, concluded the Vitaphone Prelude with "La Fiesta" as a musical prologue to *Don Juan*.

During the intermission, the lobby was filled with excited, elated and enthusiastic humanity. "Didn't believe it possible!" "Never heard anything so marvelous!" "Glorious! Beautiful! Divine!" These were some of the comments heard on all sides.

The entire New York press, motion picture executives, Wall Street financiers, all pronounced the Vitaphone the greatest achievement the world of music and art has yet known. Vitaphone had, indeed, thrilled the world!!

Following the ten-minute intermission, *Don Juan* starring John Barrymore, started. Here is, without the question of a doubt, Barrymore's greatest picture. As the great lover of women, he is handsome, fascinating, fickle, and elusive. He goes from one love affair to another as easily as the average man goes from breakfast to lunch and then to dinner.

The entire production abounds in subtle touches and situations. The sets are gorgeous, the direction brilliant and the entire production one of the finest that this season has given us.

The synchronization of film and music throughout the entire picture was so perfect that it aroused wonder and speculation in the minds of the audience. Every bit of action, every nuance was perfectly timed and not a false note struck in the entire presentation.

Sam Warner, the family's greatest enthusiast for sound, was put in charge of the project. He prepared the short films at the old Vitagraph studios in Brooklyn, New York, while Jack Warner assisted in preparing the musical track to *Don Juan* in Hollywood.

191 Kisses in Don Juan

Author unknown
Variety
AUGUST 1926

John Barrymore has established a new world's record! He is the champion kisser of all times.

In **Don Juan**, in which he is starred and which had its premiere at the Warner Theater last night, Don Juan bestowed 191 kisses on the beautiful ladies who assist him in his amorous expeditions.

These kisses were of all kinds, brands and varieties. Some were cool little pecks on the cheek, others tender touch of lips to lips, but most of them were hot and long and drew envious murmurs from the female portion of the audience. In fact, most of the osculation in the picture was of such a tempestuous nature that Barrymore was seen wiping the perspiration from his brow after several of these ardent embraces.

Behind the Scenes in Making of Warner Bros.' Don Juan

Variety
AUGUST 7, 1926

The impressive sets used in the production were as carefully designed and built as if they were going to be permanent structures. The reproduction of the Spanish-Moorish castle hall followed a careful study of the architecture of the Renaissance. Even the doors, which convey a feeling of strength and solidity, are the real things. Fifty-three of these great doors were made for the play, varying from a height of seven feet. These are all carved in the manner of the period.

An exact replica was made of the dungeons in the prison of the castle of St. Angelo, and their flooding by the River Tiber is based on an occurrence, which is historically correct. Incidentally, in filming the thrilling dungeon scene, Director Alan Crosland and his cinematographer, Byron Haskins, were caged in a heavyweight tight box with an inch-thick plate glass for the camera to photograph through. The action depicts the breaking of the wall and the flooding of the dungeon into which Don Juan had been thrown at the order of Lucretia Borgia.

It was in such fashion that obstacles were overcome and difficulties surmounted in the making of this spectacle. In another scene in the dungeon a fog was needed to convey an idea of the pestilential atmosphere of the place, which was filled with slime and seepage. This effect was obtained by using a sort of powder, which makes a heavy, thick smoke that clings to the ground. The right touch was obtained for photographic purposes, but every few minutes the entire company would make a dash outside for fresh air.

Many acts of daring occurred during the filming of the various scenes besides those, which register on the screen. In the filming of a love scene in the dressing room of Adriana (played by Mary Astor), as Don Juan came through the tall, recessed window, the enormous pane of glass shattered, showering over him. Barrymore went right on with the scene as if nothing were happening, while the cameraman ground away steadily. It was just luck that Barrymore came through the scene without harm.

"Harry Warner claims Vitaphone is something new—
the dessert in an amusement meal that has come to
deliver mostly an old favorite brand of hokum."

They Stand Together – The Four Brothers: Harry, Jack, Sam, Abe

The following article was written by C.G. DuBois, the president of the Western Electric Company; the firm behind the creation of the Vitaphone Process.

Creation of a New Art

C.G. DuBois
Variety
AUGUST 6, 1926

The preproduction of sound and scene, perfectly synchronized in the Vitaphone is not only an achievement of high scientific importance; it is an event of far-reaching significance in human affairs.

In only fifty years the telephone, the phonograph and radio have been invented, perfected and adopted into common use, all making speech, music and other sounds available to the listener far beyond reach of the original sound. So far as sound is concerned neither time nor distance longer limit us.

In later years, the art of acting, the art of photography and the device our fathers knew and the naively call the "magic" lantern, have been marvelously developed into the motion picture so that every village and hamlet in the land may be represented from it in time and space.

These two great developments have revolutionized human life, yet neither completely satisfies. It is natural to see and hear at the same time. We may and we do artificially adapt our mental processes to either effect alone but the combination of the two is what the mind instinctively seeks.

The Vitaphone does this and thereby creates a new art.

Anyone may prophesy as to just what direction its uses and effects will take as the years go on. No one can doubt the great possibilities it contains for preserving and disseminating knowledge, understanding and culture.

On behalf of the Western Electric Company, I take this opportunity to express our satisfaction that we have had a part in bringing this new art into being and our earnest hopes that it may fully develop its inherent possibilities for the benefit and pleasure of mankind.

Singers, Musicians Awaken to Chance in Motion Pictures:
Vitaphone Opens Doors to One Line of Artists
Heretofore Prevented from Contributing to Screen-
Operatic and Concert Stars to Have Opportunity

Variety
AUGUST 6, 1926

Last night's demonstration of the Vitaphone, given in conjunction with
the premiere of **Don Juan** at the Warner Theatre, New York, opens up
an amazing field of surmise and speculation. In addition to eliciting the
most enthusiastic comments from noted composers and musicians who
were in the audience and who literally were astounded at the perfect
synchronization of music and motion picture, that were heard on all
sides of many opinions regarding the future possibilities of the apparatus.

Like every other revolutionary invention, Vitaphone opens wide
many doors that have hitherto been closed. For one thing, it destroys the
barriers that have prevented the musical artist from entering the motion
picture field and puts him on a par with the dramatist and actor, who
have found the realm of the cinema highly profitable. The concert and
operatic worlds have at last been merged with that of the screen, and the
resulting sphere is as large as the universe itself.

With the established practicality of Vitaphone comes assurance that
presentations of grand opera and light opera, as well as musical revues
are made possible in all of the motion pictures theatres of the globe.
Performances such as are given in the leading opera houses can now be
reproduced in their entirety on the screen, with Vitaphone furnishing the
music in perfect synchronization with the acting.

What a real boon this will be to music lovers.

Every well-known artist who has limited his talents to the making of
phonograph records now has broader opportunity to appeal before vast
audiences, through the registration of his art for Vitaphone reproduction.

"Harry is the 'presiding genius over all their plans. It was he who visualized the great possibilities in Vitaphone when it was offered to him as an obscure invention—which most of the filmdom's other great magnates had the same chance and turned it down. Now he foresees a future for the principle that his device represents, so great that it staggers any but a great imagination. The next step", he says, "will be the actual introduction of speaking into the motion picture… the very thing many people have been waiting for."

Fairbanks, Pickford and Other Notables Slated for Discard, HM Warner Predicts

Seattle Post Intelligencer
AUGUST 26, 1926

"So far, the Vitaphone has been utilized only to augment the movies – in the way of a musical prologue and orchestration during the actual play. But this will soon develop into the use of the device to emphasize dramatic high spots in the film itself and then, the talking movie, in which all the characters will speak just as they do on the legitimate stage, will ultimately and inevitably.

But we're going a lot farther than that before we get through. We're going to bring in a new generation of film stars…"

The Bomb that Blew the Movies Upside Down

The American Magazine
APRIL 1929

"My friends, no story ever written for the screen is as dramatic as the story of the screen itself!" exclaimed Will Hays to a thrilled audience on the night of the August 6, 1926.

He was speaking of an event that was to convulse America's $8,000,000,000 moving picture industry. For, as one of the movie magnates has since more bluntly put it, "Science was about to explode a bomb under the most prosperous business our country has ever known! The bomb was the Talking Picture."

On that night, a drama was being shown on the screen of the New York movie theater, in which Mr. Hayes spoke on the same night, and still in the same Broadway theater. Another drama was taking place actually in the lives of the four men who sat well back in the audience.

Before the screen drama was ended the terrific problem that faced this little group of men would also have been solved. Whether they would be rich or bankrupt, wise men or fools, successes or failures, was being decided by the large public jury who sat about them. One of the men wiped his mouth nervously with his hand. "Maybe we'll win," he muttered.

The other three only gripped the arms of their seats more tightly and in grim silence awaited the verdict.

The men were Harry Warner, and his brothers in a film firm known as Warner Bros., who make "Vitaphone" pictures. They had sunk over $500,000 in this one picture. [**Don Juan**] They had invested nearly $10,000,000 in a gigantic gamble that the American public would like moving pictures that *talked*.

If they won, they would revolutionize moving pictures. If they won a new art would be launched. If they won, a vast population of 50,000,000 movie fans would have to be reeducated. If they won – and this they did not dare even discuss with one another – they might pull the entire industry down upon the heads of those who had so patiently built it.

They had struggled twenty years that this night might be a success. They had fought with other film firms for their own firm's very existence. They knew that America was too big to win by halfway measures.

Stars of the Metropolitan Opera Company of New York had been recorded for this momentous event. The "gamblers" had to pay another company $104,000 for permission to use the music that the stars would sing, the period of such singing being limited to one year.

And now they tensely waited. Literally they could be made or damned on the opening night by the verdict of this single New York audience. And practically every expert in America had called the effort to put talking pictures across a kind of pitiable insanity.

The theater was filled, every seat was sold and occupied. It was a curious, speculative audience, more prepared to be amused by a new scientific miracle than to be entertained by anything artistic.

At 8:30 the lights dimmed. Voices hushed. A white beam shot overhead and splashed upon the screen. A single brief title showed, then the image of a man—it was Will Hays who walked forward and began to speak.

The hush before him seemed to deepen. "The suspense was pretty tight, I tell you," laughed a friend of mine who was present that night, and knew nothing of the human drama going on behind him. "We all felt as if something could to go wrong. The machinery would break down or a crash of some sort would suddenly spoil it all."

But it didn't.

The "shadow" of Will Hays finished his "shadow speech." The audience applauded. As the clapping died away, sweet music came from the direction of the screen. Abruptly the motion picture of an orchestra making *that* music. Close-ups of famous opera-singers followed. Each was *seen* and *heard*. The illusion was complete.

When the lights went up for the intermission, the audience cheered, then gave way to a concentrated buzz of excitement. History was being made and they were there to see the event.

The second half was a conventional screen drama, also with the new talking-picture attachment. But before this stirring plot was done the little group of four who sat tensely waiting, received their verdict. The uncontrollable enthusiasm of the audience gave it: *"You win!"*

It was the first great triumph for the "Talkies," as the public instantly named the new synchronized pictures. It was a glorious tribute to the men who had backed them. It made the biggest producers in the movies sit and rub their eyes. This thing that they had one and all condemned, all except the little group we have named, was rising like one of Aladdin's genie from the lamp of a single small company and bewitching the public.

The Talkie boom was on!

"Harry Warner is a humanitarian and an idealist. His startling statement proves it: 'Vitaphone may even serve to eliminate war among the nations. We think of the film as the greatest of all the media for propaganda. We know that American movies are bearing a silent message of our progress to the people inhabiting the globe.'"

Vitaphone Thrills L.A.: Blase First-Nighters Get a
Taste of Something New and Really Worth While –
Perfect Synchronization of Sound and Motion Causes
Spectators to Gasp Sid Grauman Praised On All
Sides For His Master Stroke of Showmanship

Arthur Ungar
Variety
OCTOBER 27, 1926

Well folks, they went and did it at Grauman's Egyptian tonight! They put on something which Hollywood has been hearing about but never had the chance to hear. It was nothing more than that uncanny device— the Vitaphone. It was presented in conjunction with John Barrymore's sensational cinema, **Don Juan** and held everybody among the lucky 1,800 in the house spellbound and thrilled them as they have never been before.

New history was made in Hollywood picture annals, and it looks as though if anyone wants to keep abreast of the times when showing deluxe pictures they will have to get that Warner Brother's Vitaphone attachment. That will spell sure success and long runs, as **Don Juan** with the new device appliance operating in conjunction with it is sure to remain on Hollywood Boulevard.

Those hardboiled picture people who have been waiting to see what this thing was all about, were shown and shown aplenty. That gang of skeptics who sit on the sidelines and say, "It must have been an accident," when something good in pictures or presentations have been achieved, did not have chips on their shoulders tonight. They just let their eyes bulge out of their heads and ears strain as they never did before. They heard and saw and not once did they have an opportunity to assert themselves in a facetious manner. They found that the Warner Boys – Harry, Sam, Albert and Jack – had pulled a ten strike which marks a new turning point in the history of the motion picture and theatre entertainment.

It was just 100% plus entertainment that Sid Grauman can take all the honors for as he was the first showman on the West Coast to realize the value of the perfected Vitaphone and brought it to show his patrons as fast as he could get the device erected and going. Listening to the comment of the audience on both the Vitaphone and the picture it was a cinch to determine that the new program in the Egyptian was a sure-fire winner.

Everyone was enthusiastic about the device. They just could not grasp it all. Many expressed a desire to come and see and hear again. Really to them the installation of the Vitaphone and its operation was just as much as a mystery and novelty as was the first electric light globe that Thomas A. Edison turned out. That globe was the sensation of its day and Vitaphone proved to be the biggest sensation of the present day. Other devices have come and gone in the picture talking game, but it looks as though Vitaphone has come to stay until eternity.

Hollywood was thrown into a turmoil. If an airship had landed from Mars there could not have been more excitement. Stars tottered on their thrones. Long-term contracts became scraps of paper. Studios were shut down.

An army of extras became a howling mob of hopefuls. Maybe they could talk! Maybe their voices were better than their looks! Perhaps the new art would seize the unknown just as its infancy the old art had! Their ages ranged from fifteen to eighty. But perhaps age didn't matter in the Talkies! None knew.

There was a wild scurrying around to see how one could master the art of pronunciation. A new business sprang up in answer to the demand. All over Hollywood were shingles reading: "School of Voice Culture"; and "We Teach Dramatic Art." Their number increased until they had a separate section in the local telephone book!

Meanwhile, the battle against noise was on, that is, noise in the studios where the Talkies were being made.

This was a body blow to the red-blooded director. For years had thrived on noise. *"Music, Action, Camera!"* he had thundered for years. *"Where is that blankety-blank script!"* he loved to roar. And now they were going to choke him off!

But there was no other way. The very electro-mechanical efficiency that had made the Talkies possible, now began to make them impossible! All sorts of crazy noises were caught by the delicate ear of the recording mechanism.

Even the camera had to be squelched. Its musical whirr had not intruded before. Now it was like the rumble of an express train rushing through a tunnel!

A separate sound-proof booth was worked out. Early recording apparatus' had camera and recorder in the same booth. Now they were put far apart, but their mechanism still had to be kept perfectly synchronized.

Other noises had to be hurriedly eliminated by imposing a severe military discipline upon the whole studio.

Another unforeseen horror was the microphones through which speech or music was taken. Actors could no longer get by with pleasing gestures. They were "slaves of the mike."

Mikes had to be hung all over the place. An actor had to be sure he was in the right position for his words. If he were a foot or two to one side, his recorded voice would sound as if he were speaking from the bottom of a well.

A tough mechanical task daily tormented the studio helpers. This was the cruel necessity of keeping the camera and sound apparatus in step: *"synchronization"* it is technically called. The sound part of the mechanism was like a phonograph. It had a wax disk on which recorded the Talkie.

Speed ratios of making the two records were simple enough. The wax disk went at a speed of about 100 feet a minute under its vibrating needle. The film took about 1,440 pictures in the same period of time. But a cameraman who cranked 1,600 pictures one minute and 1,200 the next would soon make characters speaking with female voices!

"We began to wish we had never heard of talking pictures!" one of the men who worked with them in the early days feelingly told me.

"It was even worse when we realized that we had to cut and splice film in spots, and yet not break the synchronization of sound and scene."

But with the new Talkies those who made them just couldn't bring themselves to face what was to them an unsolvable problem. Then came the day of reckoning. One morning an assistant rushed up to his director waving a yellow telegraph blank.

"They've done it!" he cried.

"Done what?" he exploded nervously.

"Censored that last film!"

The director collapsed into a chair. He had been so careful, so painstakingly meticulous not to tread on anyone's toes in any of the Talkies he had made. And now some censor had said it was necessary to cut a piece out of the film!

"Throw it all away," he almost sobbed. It looked as if that were the only thing to do. You could cut film by snipping it with shears and gluing the ends together. But you couldn't do that with a wax disk – without absolutely ruining it.

There were half a dozen conferences. Wild, pleading messages were shot back and forth across the continent. But to no purpose. The censors stood their ground.

The engineers stood their ground, too. "There were limits to what science could achieve," they said curtly.

The only thing to do was to begin again – throw about $200,000 worth of production into the ashcan and make it over!

But movie producers were used to fighting. After the first shock, they lifted their bloody heads, so to speak, and put them together in an earnest huddle.

During all this technical struggle an even more vigorous battle was going on behind the scenes between those struggling to control the new Talkie industry.

When fifty movie magnates, financial heavyweights of the huge film field, began to gird their loins for battle there were seismic tremors throughout the financial world. "Vitaphone is a success, financially as well as artistically!"

A new Western Electric device was installed in 25 seats in the Warner Theatre that was reserved for the blind and hard of hearing. Telephone head pieces similar to what was used on radio instruments were invented. The wires were connected to a microphone and a monitor in the back of the stage. Speaking was employed and as the picture progressed in its plot this speaker would describe the actors, the scenes, the costumes and the action fully and clearly.

Talking to Be Inserted in Third Vitaphone Movie

Bob Reel
Film News and Reviews
MARCH 1927

I found (Harry Warner) unchanged – the same considerate gentleman-looking with far-seeing eyes through spectacles a bit misty with kindness. Great success can never mean everything to Warner. For unless I am mistaken, he has paid dearly for it, in hard work, worry and heart's blood.

Harry comes first because he is the oldest and the presiding genius over all their plans. He it was who visualized the great possibilities in Vitaphone when it was offered to him—an obscure invention. Incidentally, most of filmdom's other great movie magnates had the same chance and turned it down.

Now he foresees a future for the principle that his device represents, so great that it staggers any but a great imagination.

Warner: "The next step will be the actual introduction of speaking into the motion picture...the very thing many people have been waiting for. At first it was a question as to whether the public wanted talking movies. Now it has been proved that they want to hear certain parts of the Vitaphone program.

Thus, we will hear the characters of the cinema speak as well as the singing and playing of those on the subsidiary bill."

Reporter: With the opening of this program, the New York's major theaters will be offering Vitaphone programs. Imagine what would happen if four houses in the same city, or any other city for that matter, offered grand opera! But the number does not dismay this intrepid screen magnate in the least.

Warner: "Why should we not go on acquiring theaters in New York? The public there continues to support our bills."

Reporter: The reason that it is possible to offer an unlimited number of bills at the same time, according to Mr. Warner, is that the Vitaphone can present such a varied program. Films, vaudeville, high class music, jazz entertainment for eye, ear, heart, and mind. Where else can these elements be found together on the same bill? Then he claims, Vitaphone is something new—the dessert in an amusement meal that has come to deliver mostly an old favorite brand of hokum.

Warner: "Vitaphone may even serve to eliminate war among the nations. We think of film as the greatest of all media for propaganda. We know that American movies are bearing a silent message of our progress to the peoples inhabiting the globe. These same films may now go a step further — they may even carry an actual message through speech spoken by some character, perhaps of America's doctrines for world peace."

"If we have a message of friendship or enlightenment that can be broadcast throughout the world, maybe nations will be led to understand one another better." –Harry Warner

---

In 1927, Harry Warner was asked to speak to the Graduate School of Business Administration at Harvard University. This was one of a series of lectures presented by Hollywood executives including Joseph P. Kennedy, Will H. Hays, Adolph Zukor, Jesse Lasky, Cecil B. DeMille, Samuel Katz, Marcus Loew, and

William Fox. These series of lectures were later published in a book entitled
"The Story of Films" *in 1927.*

Harry Warner Addresses Harvard Students

MARCH 30, 1927

"The Vitaphone is, I presume, the thing that you all want to hear about, so I will step outside of formalities and try to give you a little outline of it. As preliminary and a sort of parallel case, I would like to tell you about a motion picture theatre we had in New Castle, Pennsylvania, many years ago. When the theatre was all finished, we found we had no chairs... So, we went over and engaged ninety-six chairs from a neighboring undertaker. The consequence was whenever there was a funeral we had to ask the audience to stand up. Picture that theatre with those ninety-six chairs and then picture the Roxy Theater today, and you will have an idea of the development of the motion picture industry.

It may be this thought would never have come to my mind if my brother, Sam Warner, who had been fooling around with radio stations, had not wired me one day: 'Go to the Western Electric Co. and see what I consider the greatest thing in the world.' After a while, I went and heard it and wired him back, 'I think you are right.' Had he wired me to go up and hear a talking picture I would never have gone near it, because I had heard and seen talking pictures so much that I would not have walked across the street to look at one. But, when I heard a twelve-piece orchestra on that screen at the Bell Telephone Laboratories, I could not believe my own ears. I walked in back of the screen to see if they did not have an orchestra there synchronizing with the picture. They all laughed at me. The whole affair was in a ten by twelve room. There were a lot of bulbs and working things I knew nothing about, but there was not any concealed orchestra.

The thought occurred to me that if we quit the idea of a talking picture and brought about something the motion picture theatre of the present day really needs which was music adapted to pictures, we could ultimately develop it to a point at which people would ask us for talking pictures. If I myself would not have gone across the street to see or hear a talking picture, I surely could not expect the public to. But music! That is another story. An organ playing to a picture was the thing that

I visualized. I stopped and thought a minute and said: 'Here's a theater that seats four or five thousand people, runs a motion picture, which is the most important part of the business, and neglects the most important part of the picture, which is the music. The manager plays his music as an overture and does not play it to the picture.' Take a motion picture, a silent one, and run it off. Then take the same picture and run it with an orchestra, and you will see the difference. That vision came to me. So I took it up with the head of Western Electric Company and arrived at an understanding with him. I will give our arrangement as briefly as I can.

They were to agree to discontinue the use of the name, 'talking picture' and devote their time entirely to music. Then the question came up, what is the proper method of bringing this instrument before the public? Some members of our firm were for taking a little theatre, making up a few vaudeville numbers and asking the different exhibitors throughout the country to come in and hear it. That would be a long, drawn-out process, and the objection came up that we would be competing with the 'short-reel' subject, which does not cost the theater man much, and he might say, 'Why should I throw out the short-reel subject, and take on something new which I know so little about?'

So, the battle was on and it lasted several weeks. I finally decided to do the thing on a liberal scale, because if it was worth doing at all it was worth doing well. I said to my partners: 'Let's get the greatest artist and the best orchestras in the country. Let's have confidence in this and put all our muscle behind it. We'll know the result after we have opened the first show.' I banked on the ability of the Western Electric Company with the thirty-five hundred people employed in Bell Laboratory to take care of the proper working of the instrument itself. As long as the telephone company and its subsidiaries were lending their name to an instrument, it was up to them to make sure that it was right, because they had just as much at stake as we had. While we could go broke and they could not, nevertheless the stake was there for both of us.

So, we put on a first class show and opened it to the public. The critics lauded it as a great success. Everybody talked about it but everybody still continued saying that talking pictures were not a success. Still the show went on. Now, the question arose, 'The show is open and everything is fine, but who is going to buy our machines?'

Here is the problem that we were and are confronted with. I do not want you to think for a minute that the victory has been won. New ideas do not penetrate the human mind easily as that. They take more time. We have confidence in our idea and we have put our money in it, but it still furnishes us serious problems.

The main problem is this: The people in the amusement business have developed mammoth enterprises and they have built them along certain lines. Some give just motion pictures and some motion pictures and vaudeville and some vaudeville alone. Now they say: 'We have built these institutions, and they are successful. Why should we discard any part of that which is successful to try something new?' After establishing the success of the invention, we found that we had that difficulty in front of us. I read in a magazine only yesterday that the Keith-Albee performing arts people have put a clause in their contract forbidding any actor that works for them to appear on the Vitaphone. I have gone around to the heads of several companies and tried to persuade them to participate and become a part of our company, but as yet I must admit we have not succeeded.

We cannot take defeat so easily, so we set out to prove to them that we are right. Now, if you think you're right, you cannot do wrong. So, we went out and convinced the first man that the Vitaphone was a good thing and he put in a machine. Then we opened more shows on Broadway. I will admit to you that it is not good business for a firm to open three shows on Broadway, but to convince the theater people that the Vitaphone is all right, we opened number two and number three shows and showed them just what they were doing. We wanted to prove that there was a public that wished to see good pictures with good music; that the Vitaphone helped the picture by its orchestration; and, if so, they ought to put it in. Well, we convinced them one at a time, until today, the wire I had Saturday was one hundred and forty convinced theater people. That is quite a lot...

If one hundred and fifty theatres will have these machines installed by August first, why, of course, the machine will be able to speak for itself. After that it will not be necessary, I am positive, for us to worry about its success. The theatre man is no different from any other businessman. When he sees the man around the corner doing well, he wants the same thing and he wants it on the same terms.

Now, for the benefits. We must always try to visualize these, because that which is visualized is that which we can do. And visualization of the final result helps us over the discouraging moments. I was very sorry a couple of weeks ago to read the headlines of a New York newspaper, which said that Edison called the talking pictures a failure. You know it is not so comfortable to have your life's wealth invested in a thing, which such a great authority as Edison says cannot succeed. I wrote an answer and pointed out that they may have been a failure fifteen years ago but if Edison himself looked at his own bulb of that period and compared it with the bulb of today he would not recognize it...

Young men like you must never get discouraged when others say that some enterprise in which you are interested will not be a success. You must be satisfied in your own mind, as I was about the Vitaphone when I saw that it would bring to the small hamlet and the small theatre the same performance that the big theatre has. There is no reason why an instrument of this kind cannot bring into a town of ten thousand with a theatre of eight hundred seats the same show that is being performed in a theater of five thousand seats in a big city.

But the introduction of any novelty like that takes time, and just how it is going to be done I cannot yet say. There are a great many problems to solve in the distributing end of the Vitaphone. You have to deal with the big theater and you have to deal with the small one. The problems are many and different, but I am sure we will ultimately overcome them all, particularly as we have the assistance of the Western Electric Company, whose name the machine carries.

There are other new inventions, or new methods, that are required in the picture business. Let me tell you about one. About three years ago I saw them making pictures with a carbon light. A set the size of this room would take possibly forty or fifty electricians to light it. I asked why they could not get a bulb that would do the work. Everybody said it could not be done. Last Saturday we finished our first picture with an incandescent lamp doing the work. Now, that is quite a step forward in the motion picture business.

Suppose you had to light up an enormous street scene and you had to have two or three hundred electricians. Instead of that, you can do it with buttons at one desk. I saw some of the reels of the first picture, and the lighting is better than with carbon because it is softer. You cannot get as soft a light with carbon as you can get with the regular bulb. You can divide your light better and when you work with the carbon you have to work with more powerful electricity. There you have an important technical advance in the making of motion pictures....

The big job before us is to provide the proper kind of entertainment through the Vitaphone. We are confident people will go to hear the Vitaphone but we know the proper kind of entertainment must be supplied, if it is going to be a great success."

"The reasons new developments are so hard to put over, no matter how good they are, is because of the inborn cowardice of average human beings. They are afraid to change their accustomed ways." –Harry Warner

---

Harry Warner told his brother Jack that "he desperately wanted the rights to **The Jazz Singer.**" *The actor George Jessel said that Harry told him, "It would be a good picture to make for the sake of racial tolerance, if nothing else." Other Jewish moguls shied away from their Judaism and hid it.*

This coming year we are to make three pictures in which the Vitaphone will play an important part. For instance, in the making of a scene in which a stage forms part of the view and the actors are seen playing, we intend to bring out the actors' singing and the actual performance of each person on the stage. Our first picture embodying that feature will be **The Jazz Singer** with Al Jolson. Then we are going to perform a wedding ceremony. As you see it today, a wedding performed on the screen takes place in complete silence. Nobody knows what the priest or the preacher or the rabbi has said. We will actually perform a wedding ceremony and try to make it as real as life...

Here is another point to consider. Take a theatre that does $30,000 worth of business this week. The owner has a big orchestra and a big prologue, and it is very expensive. He thinks he sees where he can save money. Next week he gives the same kind of a show with a new picture, but no music and he does only $18,000 worth of business. What made the difference? Evidently it was the music. Did he save anything? That is just the question.

In my experience it is the picture that counts, and you have to do everything possible to help the picture. Now, if an orchestra will help the picture, that is the thing that you should have, but unfortunately you cannot afford to play an orchestra with a picture five times a day....

Machines will have to be sold one at a time. The reason new developments are so hard to put over, no matter how good they are, is because of the inborn cowardice of average human beings. They are afraid to change their accustomed ways…

Another example is: Take the people in the vaudeville business. What did they say of motion pictures when those were a novelty? They laughed at them. 'Why, we've nothing to worry about.' And the people on the legitimate stage, what did they say? 'Motion pictures will never take the place of legitimate acting.' But they waited too long. The picture today has certainly taken the place of vaudeville. While both are used in combination, it is the picture that brings in the business. So, I only hope the men who are waiting do not wait too long with the Vitaphone. I am trying to persuade them to hurry a little, trying to convey to them my own enthusiasm and my own confidence…"

Question Period:

Mr. Kennedy: Mr. Warner, I have been handed several questions which I think those that are here would like to have you answer.

Mr. Warner: "I shall be very glad to."

Mr. Kennedy: Do you lease or sell the Vitaphone?

Mr. Warner: "I said that was a problem that we are confronted with. At this particular time this is what we do. We take the cost of the machine and we lease it on that basis to the man who runs the theatre. If he does not want to pay cash, he pays in installments extending over twelve months; possibly twenty-five per cent cash and the balance divided over twelve months. Then we charge him a tax of 10 cents a seat a week. If the theater has two thousand seats, he pays us $200 a week for forty weeks in a year, figuring that he may close his theatre twelve weeks in the summertime. That does not mean that that is the way it is ultimately going to be done, because I personally believe that the man who has a small theater in a small town will not be able to pay that much money. If he has nine hundred seats and we charge him $90 a week in addition to the price of the machine, I think ultimately the burden will prove too heavy, and we shall have to modify our policy to meet the requirements of the situation."

Mr. Kennedy: What approximately does it cost to install?

Mr. Warner: "We have got it down to the cheapest figure. In a theatre of nine hundred or one thousand seats, it costs $16,000."

<u>Mr. Kennedy</u>: Describe how it was first introduced.

<u>Mr. Warner</u>: "When we got this Vitaphone first, we decided to do it on a large scale. We were at that time starting to make pictures with John Barrymore, and the first picture we made on a large scale, much larger than we intended was ***Don Juan*** with John Barrymore."

<u>Mr. Kennedy</u>: Describe how your method differs from the Fox method, the other socalled "talking picture?"

<u>Mr. Warner</u>: "In the Fox method you take both picture and music on a film instead of taking the picture on a film and the music on a record and running both off so that they correspond exactly. When we first started, this was the way the mechanical end operated. A camera and a Vitaphone instrument were placed in one little soundproof room. They were connected with a rod and cogwheels on each side and both worked automatically. But the grind of these two wheels was heard in the audience. After we go the picture people in it, they developed it so that the camera could work on one floor and the recording man on another. We now have them six stories apart, and in the building we have bought in New York, where all our work will be done. It's known as the Cosmopolitan Studios. We shall be able to operate still farther away.

The time is not far in the distant when you will be able to see and hear the inauguration of the next President. His address to the American people will be spread everywhere through the theatres on the Vitaphone perfectly because by that time we shall be able to record in New York the address delivered in Washington.

We have developed our machine with an extra attachment that costs less than a thousand dollars, which enables us to use also the Fox Movietone method. So that a theatre putting in a Vitaphone can use either method now used by us or the one on the film. Remember that the other system does all the work by a ray of light that penetrates and marks the film. I heard a demonstration not long ago, and it is very good. In order to protect ourselves in the future, we obtained all the rights and interest in the Movietone method.

This arrangement was a mutual one. Mr. Fox also has the right to manufacture his own numbers and his own pictures to be run on our machine. We gave him the right to manufacture either way, so that he can manufacture pictures by installing our apparatus or continue the way he is doing at the present time."

<u>Question</u>: Do you propose to see the Vitaphone at cost or less than

cost and make the money from the use of it, or do you propose to make the profit on the sale of the Vitaphone?

Mr. Warner: "There are several things to consider there, if there is a competitive machine that may influence our policy. As yet, I do not know of any effective competition. There are a great many machines being demonstrated, but one thing is lacking and that is amplification. There is only one company that has the telephone, and the telephone amplification is that which is used with the Vitaphone. I think ultimately the seat tax will be changed, but it is a little bit too new to say just how…

We honestly believe the Vitaphone is going to do more good for humanity than anything else ever invented.

We all know that if you and I can talk to one another, we can understand one another. (If Lincoln's Gettysburg Address could be repeated all over the world, maybe the world at large would understand what America stands for.) We think that people read and know a lot of things, but when we get out into the world and see the masses of people and find out how many are working so hard to earn a living that they have not time to read, then we realize how much remains to be done in the way of bringing knowledge to them.

If we have a message of friendship or enlightenment that can be broadcast throughout the world, maybe the nations will be led to understand one another better. The Vitaphone can do all that. That is a limited number of people who can go to the opera and pay seven or eight dollars to hear the great operatic artists of the world, but there are millions who cannot. Some of them want to hear good music, and the Vitaphone makes that possible. These are the benefits and potentialities of this invention that honestly and sincerely make us fight on for it. If the issue was just money alone, I give you my word as a man that the money I have put into the Vitaphone already all four Warner brothers could live the rest of their lives without worrying."

Sam Warner and William Koenig

On October 6ᵗʰ 1927 The Jazz Singer was released!

The Jazz Singer wasn't the first talking picture, but it had an actor with an electric personality—Al Jolson. It leveraged the convergence of technology, and studio ambition.

Beginning in 1896, dozens of systems were developed and promptly failed. Most tried to synchronize a flat cylinder record to a separate projector. When Sam Warner, the most technical visionary of the Warner brothers, was bowled over by Bell Labs' demonstration of a new sound film system in 1925, he saw those technical roadblocks evaporate.

Using one motor to drive both the projector and the turntable holding the 16" soundtrack disk, the Vitaphone system also used state-of-the-art electrical sound recording, and could fill theatres with natural sound via newly developed loudspeakers. To give Warner Bros. a step up in the Hollywood hierarchy, audience response to the talking/singing shorts preceding their first Vitaphone feature, **Don Juan,** changed all that.

Production of **The Jazz Singer** began in early summer 1927 with the shooting of location scenes in New York. Meanwhile, the Sunset Boulevard studio was wired for sound. Jolson's singing and talking sequences were shot over nine consecutive days beginning on August 17, 1927. It took 8 weeks to shoot **The Jazz Singer**, including the sound sequences. The movie contained barely two-minutes worth of synchronized talking. Most of it was improvised by Al Jolson.

Al Jolson's contract for his 1926 Vitaphone short specifically states he will sing and speak. Nevertheless, his lines about moving to the Bronx are not in the script, so he probably came up with the dialog himself. Reviews were decidedly mixed, with many commenting on Jolson's "hammy" performance, and the "New York Herald Tribune" calling it "A pleasant enough sentimental orgy."

The production cost was $422,000 which was a large sum for Warner Bros. The movie produced $3 million in profits, saving the brothers from bankruptcy and launched Warner Bros. into being a major studio.

The transition to sound, driven by the film's success, drove Warner's expansion, purchases of hundreds of theatres and First National studios, and its stock price from $21 to $132 per share.

Note: The brothers' greatest triumph was not experienced by the family as Sam Warner passed away the day before the premiere of **The Jazz Singer** on October 5th 1927. Sam had checked himself in to the hospital to treat his chronic sinus troubles. After four surgeries to remove the infection in his nose and brain caused by splinters of bone from an earlier broken nose, he slipped into a coma and died of pneumonia caused by sinusitis.

All the Brothers Were Valiant: Harry and Sam, Abe and Jack Have Never Repudiated Their Own Declaration of Independence

Dorothy Donnell
Motion Picture
FEBRUARY 1929

Notice: Warner Brothers Is Not For Sale.

One week not long ago, all the motion picture trade papers carried this advertisement. Behind these seven terse words lies the greatest drama of

Hollywood, a drama greater than any celluloid struggles and gelatin epics the Warners have ever filmed.

Two years ago, it was whispered, with that pleased expression with which Hollywood passes along bad news, that the Warner Brothers were on the verge of bankruptcy. Two months ago, the same whispers said, they refused twenty million dollars for their company. They could sell now, retire and live like rich men, but they're not going to. They are going to make pictures.

Warner Brothers, 1923: the butt of good-natured raillery. The local joke of vaudeville teams ("Varner Broders makes it a great success mitt the movink pichers, aint' it, Abie?" "How's that, Mawruss?" "Yell, vend y come oud here dey got forty cents by their name, end now dey owe forty millions. Dot's success Abie.") Warner Bros., the poor suckers who imagined they could make independent pictures without asking the consent of the big boys. Going to make movies eh? And what are they going to use for money? Ha, ha, ha!

When Harry was asked how he raised the money he did? His response was, "It was a little like the fellow who asked every girl to kiss him."

Interviewer: Weren't you slapped sometimes?

Harry: "Yes, I'd get slapped occasionally, but sometimes they'd kiss me. I asked everyone I knew for the loan of money. A lot of them turned me down. But enough let me have the money to carry on."

Warner Bros., 1929: a studio of white stone, built on classic lines. Two powerful radio masts broadcasting K.F.W.B. into the listening air. A great theater with long lines of fans waiting to see the new talking pictures the Warners have fathered. A huge tie-up with First National and the Stanley company of America to open thousands of other theaters to their pictures. The biggest producers in Hollywood murmur the name enviously, bitterly and reverently, "Warner Brothers – the lucky guys!"

Like Lindbergh, none of them ever uses the word "I" in conversation. It is always "We." "We did such and such. We think so and so." Even Sam Warner, who died suddenly, is still included in that loyal family, "we." There are still four Warner Brothers.

Pearl and Ben Warner

In Each They Trust

There is something old-world about this loyalty to the family clan. Perhaps Benjamin Warner, the Polish shoemaker, and his wife who immigrated with him to America, instilled this solidarity of interests into their children. At any rate, the word "mine" was never heard in that household. Everything from a toy to a coat was "ours." The father pawned his one fine possession, a watch he had brought with him from Poland. It is only within the last few years that the Warner Brothers have bothered with the details of legal partnership. They worked up together from nickelodeons to a motion picture business worth millions. They made and lost several fortunes on the way up without a single legal document to show who owned what.

In Sam Warner's will after provision was made for his wife and baby daughter, the remainder of his fortune went to his brothers. "For," the document says simply, "the Warners always stick together and trust each other." This mutual admiration and lack of jealousy perhaps explains their astonishing career which began in 1903.

The three elder boys all had jobs. But even in those early days they had a marked prejudice against working for other people. Sam, who was a man-of-all-work in the local amusement park, brought out his savings; the others emptied their pockets, the father of the family was called in, and the first Warner Brothers venture into the field of motion pictures was launched.

"We've never left the business since," says Jack Warner with the flashing smile that has always been just as ready when Hollywood joked about their struggles. "Of course, in those days they had to keep yanking me away from the show to go to school.

Twenty-five years ago, motion pictures were the pariahs of the amusement world. Real actors scorned to work in them. Theatrical magnates refused to take them seriously. 'They're just a novelty,' they said, 'they won't last.'"

There were four people who thought differently: Harry, Sam, Abe, and Jack Warner, believed in the future of these splotched, blurred, flickering movies. They were willing to back up their belief with their time. They were the first to conceive the idea of distributing pictures to the different nickelodeons in their vicinity. But just when they had begun to make money from the Duquesne Amusement Supply Company, the producers decided to distribute their own films and put them out of business.

Cans of their film were delayed at the laboratory or lost in transit. But their greatest handicap was lack of distributing organization to release their pictures. And one morning Hollywood woke up to find the headlines of the morning papers flaunting the news, "Warner Bros. Buys Vitagraph." It was the writing on the wall. But some movie executives have never learned to read.

They Take up Talkies

Warner Bros. became a force to be reckoned with in the movie world. But they still had a hard struggle before them. The money they made went back into their business. The four brothers themselves worked without ceasing and lived with their families in a simplicity strange to Hollywood.

Then the Western Electric Company perfected an odd-looking little device on which they had been working silently for nine years. It was offered to most of the big motion picture companies and rejected.

"Talking motion pictures?" scoffed the big boys. "Nothing to them. People don't want their pictures to talk."

Warner Bros. owned a controlling right to Vitaphone, the first practical device for synchronizing sound with motion pictures.

Contentedly unconscious of the revolution in store for them the big boys of Hollywood watched with tolerant amusement as Warner Bros. made the first sound picture. Even when **Don Juan**, with full orchestration by the New York Symphony orchestra, was released, they showed no excitement. But when the executives of Hollywood sat at the premiere of **The Jazz Singer** and watched and heard Al Jolson on the screen before them, the unwelcomed suspicion began to creep over them that Warner Bros., the subjects of their wit for so long had stolen a march on them.

The next step forward on the part of the Warners was to acquire a controlling interest in First National Pictures, with its great stars and huge plant, and its three thousand theaters. Then doing the same with the Stanley Company of America, which owned 275 first-class theaters.

The Warner's family loyalty, a constant that carried them from the smoky calcium-lit tent show to the white stone temple on Sunset Blvd. with the words "Warner Bros. Presents" leaping in letters of fire along the facade by night remained with them still.

The cars they drove were perhaps a trifle more expensive. They built a fine home for their father and mother, and their own ways of living reflect their new prosperity, but the Warners were still working and saving. They could have sold out for twenty million, but they didn't. Pictures are their racket.

"Courage to fight against convention and ascend above life's ordinary limitations is always bubbling to the surface of the human race. But the usual impulse is toward security, and the innovator is often distrusted." –Harry Warner

---

In 1927 there were 157 theaters wired for sound. By 1929 there were 8,000. In 1928, Warner Bros. moved the studio to Burbank and by 1929 posted profits of $14 million.

Abe

In 1929, Abe Warner spoke to the press while sitting in his office on Eighth Avenue in New York:

"It was Sam whose interest in everything mechanical turned our attention first to sound pictures. And we've made millions. But that doesn't bring Sam back.

The three of us who are left will carry on, and I believe we will always accomplish more work in one day than any other trio of men will in three, not because we are smarter, but because we trust each other implicitly and don't have to waste time with petty executive jealousies.

Even our parents are still working. We built them a fine home out in Hollywood where they can lean back and take it easy. But they've worked so long that now they can't get out of the habit, and every day they drive over to the studio and keep an eye on things. Papa is seventy-two years old but he is still strong and healthy and drives his own car.

As I look back, if I have any regrets, it is that we brothers didn't get more education. Most of us stopped in grammar school. I had one year of high school because I played football. But often when I have to get up to address conferences, employee's organizations and the like, I wish I had the gift of eloquence and the training that comes from a University education. Perhaps I could reach my men better."

The Miracle a Three Years Achievement

Harry M. Warner
The Daily Film Renter
JANUARY 1, 1930

"Talking films have passed their experimental stage, and definitely taken their permanent place in the entertainment world. Even in our wildest dreams my brothers and I could not have foreseen the tremendous strides, which this most important addition to the silent screen has made in so comparatively short a time.

It is only three years since, *The Jazz Singer*, the first talking picture, was shown in New York, and caused an upheaval in this industry which even we could not imagine possible.

After the success of *The Jazz Singer* we were encouraged to make bolder experiments. *The Singing Fool*, which made box office history, and blazed the trail of talking pictures throughout the world, has proved a mascot to everyone who has dealt with it.

Exhibitors did not know the capacity of their houses until they played *The Singing Fool*. Music publishers had no idea that any song could become as popular as "Sonny Boy." The Gramophone companies are still turning out colossal quantities of "Sonny Boy" records, and more copies of the book have been sold than of any previous best seller.

Many popular and successful singing, talking, and dancing pictures have been made since *The Singing Fool*, and the next milestone on the road to progress has been reached with the use of Technicolor, a process by which everything is screened in natural colors, flesh tints, flowers, the beautiful gowns, and interior and exterior sets, which helps to add realism and life to talking pictures, and charms the eye as well as the ear.

In the very near future, it will be just as unusual to see black and white films as it is now to see silent pictures. It seems queer now when people open their mouths and say nothing, and soon it will be just as unusual to see women in black and white frocks when they are so much more attractive in rich and beautiful colors.

The first all-color film, *On with the Show*, was recently shown at the Tivoli; the latest Technicolor production, *Gold Diggers of Broadway*, opened at the Regal on December 28, and there is no doubt that this will firmly establish natural color and prove its introduction to be as epoch-making as sound.

In *Disreali*, we made a talking picture about the great British statesman, with an English cast, headed by the inimitable George Arliss, and in this production we hope we have proved that it is possible to make an artistic as well as commercial success.

Show of Shows, which has just opened in New York, and will shortly be seen in London, is the most ambitious entertainment yet made. It has seventy-seven stars, and one thousand Hollywood beauties. There has never before been anything like it. It is one hundred shows in one, and in its opulent variety embodies everything from Shakespeare to super-jazz.

Each new production that we have made has in some way been an improvement on all previous productions. We have learned the business of talking pictures more quickly and successfully than we had dared to hope.

Through the unlimited possibilities of the talking screen, we have been instrumental in introducing the best artists in every branch of entertainment.

The best talent in the amusement world is now working for pictures. Musicians get a wider field for their music when it becomes popular through the screen and famous actors, actresses, and producers reap the rewards of their work in thousands of theaters throughout the world. If they are good they can bring fortune to thousands of boxoffices. The success of a star in talking pictures is, today, the highest pinnacle that can be reached in the entertainment world, and, for that reason, more and more artistic talent is ready and willing to come our way.

With the aid of Vitaphone picture-goers in London, we are able to enjoy the performances of the stars in New York, and the people of small towns have the greatest artists and the work of the best producers in the world brought within their own small sphere.

It took twenty years to develop the silent screen, and three years to bring it color and sound to its present perfection. When you realize that you must also take into consideration the amount of research, money and thought that has resulted in the colored talking motion picture and impress on the picture-going public that they are getting all this for the same price of admission they paid to see silent films.

As long as exhibitors endeavor to make every new cinema that is built more comfortable and more artistic than any that already exists; as long as everyone connected with each new film that is made strives for something better and something different, we will continue to attract the people who are tired by their daily work into the cinemas for mental and physical relaxation.

Amusement is necessary, not a luxury, and we put forth every effort to provide the kind of entertainment that will lift people out of their everyday life and never get into a rut.

If talking pictures have done nothing else, they have caused us all to think and act quickly.

We had made silent pictures as big as it was possible to do and the addition of sound has brought in many other changes and improvements that have given the screen a new lease on life.

It is interesting to watch the birth and growth of this new art. As each production is finished, it inspires us to attempt more ambitious subjects and our plans for the future grow so fast and so vast that it is difficult for us to think too far ahead.

The whole outlook of the film industry has changed in the last year. It started with colossal changes in the studio. My brother Jack knows all about that, but he keeps smiling. Then the whole system of renting was changed, and now the exhibitor who has moved with the times is reaping the reward of progress."

"The success of a picture is not only measured in dollar and cents returned but in the worth of the principles it illustrates." –Harry Warner

---

Technical Progress

In this article, Harry Warner speculates on the future of motion pictures, including his thoughts on three-dimension, which wouldn't become popular for two more decades. He mentions a "stereopticon," sometimes call a "magic lantern," which is a projector with two lenses, usually one above the other. These devices date back to the mid-19th century and were a popular form of entertainment and education before the advent of moving pictures.

Warner Reveals Inside Story of Talkie Inception

The Motion Picture
FEBRUARY 3, 1930

"The next five years will make the motion picture miracles of the past decade, vivid as they have been, seem only a preparatory period. The absolute perfection of synchronization is here. While we are bringing the present improved inventions to a constantly higher plane of performance, the mechanical brains of the producing companies are concentrating on such problems as full natural color and the three-dimensional film. The latter will make the screen seem not a flat surface, but a complete room or countryside, with a perspective in all its true values. A sculptural quality will be added to movement, sound, and color. The stereopticon of childhood days is to undergo a magical transformation.

The Motion Picture industry, beginning in 1922 when it sought the service of Mr. Will H. Hays as a channel of contact and information with responsible public groups, has never been content with a box office standard of success. We have tried consistently to make pictures better than they had to be from a selling standpoint. We have sought advice and counsel from hundreds of religious, civic and educational leaders as to the content and treatment of our screen stories, and we have listened with thoughtful consideration to every criticism and suggestion from sincere and intelligent sources. We have put the facilities of the industry at the disposal of all those socially minded groups which have demonstrated willingness to work toward the enlistment of public support for the best pictures. What other industry has done this? I believe the attitude of the industry toward its public and the processes we have used to translate that attitude into action constitute the most distinguished experiment in human relations, which any business has ever undertaken.

Today pictures are wholesome and useful to the community. You do not have to take my word for it. During the past two years many scientists, in many countries, have made psychological tests of the effects of American made motion pictures on human behavior and have found those effects to be salutary. Such a condition could not have come to pass without effort. It will not be maintained or improved without further effort. We are ready to go forward with the best available thought and counsel to the further improvement of the service of motion pictures to the public."

"An ever-present duty to educate, stimulate and demonstrate the fundamentals of free speech, religious tolerance, freedoms of speech, freedom of press, freedom of assembly and the greatest possible happiness for the greatest possible numbers is the obligations of a producer." –Harry Warner

"Future Developments" Lecture

MARCH 30TH 1927

Harry believed "Visualization of the final result helps one over the discouraging moments. You must never get discouraged when others say that some enterprise in which you are interested will not be a success. We all know that if you and I can talk to one another, we can understand one another. If Lincoln's Gettysburg address could be repeated all over the world, maybe the world at large would understand what America stands for. We think that people read and know a lot of things, but when we get into the world and the masses of people and find out how many are working so hard to earn a living that they have not time to read, then we realize how much remains to be done in the way of bringing knowledge to them.

"We must always try to visualize the benefits of something we believe in, because that which is visualized is that which we can do. And visualization of the final results helps us over the discouraging moments." –Harry Warner

Warner Defends Films Showing Gangster Life

Author unknown
The Boston Post
JUNE 5, 1932

"Gangster pictures are not responsible for the wildness of youth nor are there too many gangster pictures. Gangster pictures properly presented should have a good effect. They are intended to point the lesson that crime does not pay. With proper home training they should assist."

Warner Brothers' Crusade Against the Third Reich: A study of Anti-Nazi Activism and Film Production

"Hollywood will fail in its most important duty in trying times if it does not present an honest and forthright collective picture of American life, manners, and privileges. A truthful picture of the American background is added assurance to a troubled world that our country will protect its rights and liberties while demonstrating the advantages of a democratic form of government. Accidentally and purposely we are advertising America to a world that is obviously a little weary of trouble. I am more than ever convinced that we have a double duty to perform. We must sell America while we entertain the world."

Sin Seeing Movies Denied

JULY 21, 1934

Harry M. Warner believes, "It is going a bit too far to make going to the movies a sin."

Warner, president of Warner Brothers First National Pictures, said he had not planned to say anything about the film clean-up move at the studio luncheon given for Postmaster General Farley here yesterday, but he was led to it by Rupert Hughes, the writer.

Hughes declared, somewhat facetiously that "all the sin in the world had been heaped on Hollywood's shoulders." Following him Warner said, "Many faults could be found with any industry, if one wants to look for faults and it is an unfortunate mistake to judge an entire industry by the faults of a few. It is going a bit too far to make going to theaters a sin."

Warner added, more or less humorously, the suggestion that Postmaster Farley issues postage stamps bearing some of the film stars' pictures and charges an extra cent for them to create a fund to aid those who might be thrown out of work if the theater ban idea spreads.

"Gangster pictures properly presented should have a good effect. They are intended to point the lesson that crime does not pay. With proper home training, they should assist…" –Harry Warner

---

Excerpts From a Speech Given at KFWB
to Warner Brothers Employees

HARRY M. WARNER

1935

All of you know that the last five years of these ten past have been very hard and struggling ones. The question of being a president of a company today is only good if all of those that are with the company are working in harmony and looking forward to the future, and the good that the future has in store for us and not always think of the past, because most of us if we thought of the past wouldn't get very far in the future.

It's just ten years ago that through this station, KFWB, talking pictures were made possible. Many of you have possibly wondered how talking pictures came about, so I'll let you in on a little secret. Ten years ago, while building this station, my brother Sam phoned me and said he was told by some of the men working in the constructing of this station that there's an apparatus I should see. And after seeing it, I then made up my mind that through this instrument talking pictures would be possible. In fact, at that time, it was my opinion that talking pictures would only come about by public demand.

It was the music of the instrument that I saw that attracted me mostly. Beyond that I was attracted by the screen being used as our future education, because through the screen you could educate. What was impossible to do with the silent picture was possible to perform by this instrument, which was soon to be a fact.

I presume that many of you who see a picture on the screen today will never realize the struggle, the torture that we went through in order to make this instrument a success.

When I myself sit in a theater and see a picture today, and think back of what I first saw, believe me, many a time I walk out of the theater with tears in my eyes. Because when you find a dream realized, and you know that no dream such as mammoth as that one was to undertake was done easy—nothing comes easy.

I do hope that you will all enjoy the performance this evening, and I hope and pray for the health of all those of our company, and a successful future. And I do hope that we will continue, and in the course of times as I can see it before me, the world will be a better place to live in than it is in the present. So let us live in the future, and radio and talking pictures hand in hand will develop to a point where the dreams of others may come true."

Harry Warner Denies Films Cause Crimes

Universal Service
FEBRUARY 10, 1936

"People who spend their time fighting the pictures could spend it better fighting the slums. Criminals breed in poverty-stricken slum districts, not in moving picture theaters.

I would guarantee you there are at least as many criminals who have never or seldom been to the movies, as there are criminals who are movie-goers. I don't think there is any connection between moving pictures and crime.

The causes of crime are what they always have been, poverty, neglect and bad environment.

"Today, pictures have become an even more important factor in world betterment. Pictures can no longer be regarded merely as entertainment. They have an undeniable influence on morals and living conditions." –Harry Warner

---

Initiative

By Harry M. Warner
MARCH 12, 1937

"Courage to fight against convention and ascend above life's ordinary limitations is always bubbling to the surface of the human race. The great poets, the great playwrights, the magnificent artists of the Renaissance, all underwent a period of condemnation – the condemnation which so frequently comes to the new and untried. But scorn and even downright hostility have never been able to still the pens and brushes that have something important to tell the world. There are no chains which can shackle genius and initiative for so long, and surely it is better so. For genius and initiative, whether in individual cases sound or unsound, are the stimulants, which keep our minds from retrogression. Ideas cradled in public disrepute have time and time again combined to change the face of earth, to man's ultimate gain.

Today initiative is as essential on the lower levels as in the stratosphere where genius lives and in the business world where men with novel ideas are no longer regarded as suspect. An employee who waits to be told what to do is in the long run is merely waiting for dismissal. When we hire a worker in our business whether a great actor or the humblest laborer we set a market price on the least that we expect from him. If he exceeds our expectations, our enthusiasm is boundless.

Sound ideas and the energy to execute those ideas are the escalators of which an employee rises automatically to success. No employer refuses to pay liberally for initiative. It is the one irreplaceable ingredient in progress. Without it, the doors of any business would be closed in a few short months.

Sometimes a definite pattern of life, whatever its apparent advantages, can be a potent danger to a man's advancement. The maintenance of the status quo in industry or politics or in a nation is as impossible of achievement as the prolongation of an April day. The sun will not wait, nor will the world. Empires, religions, and great industrial establishments alike have toppled into oblivion for lack of elasticity to move with changing times. A man who holds to a set pattern, who fails to realize that a blend of initiative and tenacity is indispensable, wakes one morning to find himself out of step with an era which has long since passed him by. Hardening of the intellectual arteries is a dangerous ailment, both to its possessor and to humanity at large. Petrified trees maintain the status quo, but they build no houses.

America was carved out of the wilderness by initiative—an initiative forged in lonely pioneer fires and tempered on the expanding hearths of industry. As long as it remains our heritage there can be no closed frontiers in all the Western World."

"I selected film because I wanted to educate people. I have faith in the mission of film. The film will establish understanding amongst the nations and create peace on Earth. We are seeking an Earth connection." –Harry Warner

Harry Receiving Award

Mr. Warner, A Friend of France and Justice
La Cinematographic Francaise

APRIL 15, 1937

We had an agreeable surprise in interviewing Mr. Harry M. Warner.

Too many representatives of these American movie magnates show us faces filled with so little friendliness and with so much self-sufficient pride that one thinks: "Decidedly, what a repugnant people! Only money means anything to them, and as for education, they haven't even an ounce of it!

And one thinks so when one sees that these representatives, one installed in France, where they take our money, have no love for our country. Lucky are we they do not hate us!"

But, double contrast: Mr. Warner loves money less than idea, and our country, where his is a chevalier of honor, he loves more than any other.

Mr. Warner told us very many nice things, which touched us, about Pasteur, the life of Zola, our great writer, whose life is going to be produced on the screen with those traits which are well-adapted to make ideas of justice, triumph; about European peace; about love that men should bear one another. Briefly, a language, which is not usually heard in the heart of cinema.

"When we made this picture, we didn't consider money. We know that it is difficult to get people to see and take an interest in that which educates them, but in spite of this, we took up this film. We must show the people the good and noble things in life." – Harry Warner about *The Story of Louis Pasteur*

The Warner Brothers: Enthroned by an Old Revolution, Harry and Abe and Jack Still Cherish Liberty, Economy, Fraternity. The Formula Earned the Biggest Movie Company $6,000,000 Net Last Year

Fortune Magazine
DECEMBER 1937

Harry M. Warner, its President and boss, explains the ten-year boom of Warner Bros. Pictures, Inc., from a rank outsider to the biggest thing in show business by telling you that he, Sam, Abe and Jack have always been great dreamers. As you reach for your hat, he detains you with a leer and some such succinct enlargement as this: "Listen, a picture, all it is an expensive dream from $700,000 to $1,500,000."

Which explains a lot, though not everything. Warner Bros. has larger gross assets ($177,500,000) than any other movie company. It has been among the giants for nine years now, so that a quick reference to *The*

Jazz Singer, whose unexpected success found Warner Bros. with a long head start in the talking-picture field, no longer suffices to dismiss its curious primacy. People in show business, by and large, are inclined to resent the Warners. Many of Hollywood's first citizens, especially over at the Metro-GoldwynMayer studio think that Harry's cut-rate dreaming is the worst possible formula for making pictures. And yet by all movie standards Hollywood's box offices and the critics agree that Warner Bros. is conceded to make very good pictures indeed.

This is all the more aggravating to Hollywood because the Warner studio, besides lacking a proper disregard for production costs, is conspicuously without that other prime necessity, a producing "genius." Warner used to have one of these in Darryl Zanuck, but he left in 1933 to join 20th Century Pictures and later to merge with Fox, where, the local wits have it, he is currently sitting on the Blarney stone of Hollywood.

Zanuck has never been officially replaced at Warner and the studio continues in the hands of a somewhat witty penny watcher, Jack Warner, his methodical assistant, Hal Wallis, and half a dozen almost anonymous supervisors.

And yet the Warner product, as its pictures are collectively known, have been getting better, not worse, ever since Zanuck left. The inexpensive topical stories that Zanuck so successfully snitched from the day's headlines (***Doorway to Hell***, ***Public Enemy***) are still pouring from Burbank in a uniformly profitable stream (***G-Men***, ***Black Legion***, ***Marked Woman***, ***China Clipper***).

But furthermore, in pictures like ***Black Fury*** (mine labor trouble), ***They Won't Forget*** (sectional prejudice in the Deep South), and ***The Life of Emile Zola*** (Zola's complacency is shaken when Jewish officer Alfred Dreyfus is wrongfully imprisoned.)

Warner has touched movie critics and fans on a nerve that had almost been atrophied by the average producer's chronic cynicism—the nerve that quickens to serious social issues. When we examine Harry's subtle and race-conscious mind, Warner is the only major studio that seems to know or care what is going on in America besides pearl-handled gunplay, sexual dalliances and the giving topcoats to comedy butlers.

In Wall Street, meanwhile, the Warner paradox has a different twist. In the big three-way movie consolidations of the twenties, when almost every studio of importance was swallowing or being swallowed by a country-wide distributing system and chain of theaters, the Warner acquisitions were conspicuously late, hasty, and gluttonous. Its bankers were those famous optimists, Goldman, Sachs, whose name became a gag synonym for New Era finance, and its particular financial adviser was Goldman, Sach's most optimistic partner, Waddill Catchings himself. A structure reared under such auspices, you would suppose, would be among the first to collapse in The Depression. The almost comical way in which the brothers hunched forward together in their oversized golden saddle seemed to betoken an early fall. Having earned what was then the record movie net of $17,000,000 in 1929, Warner Bros. piled up losses of $31,000,000 in the four years in 1931 through 1934. Litigious stockholders tried to put the brothers in the street and a federal antitrust suit threatened to put Harry in jail. "Management has shown less than average acumen," said *Barron's Weekly* as late as 1935. And yet Warner Bros. has been the only big theatre-owning company, again expecting M-G-Ms parent, Loew's, Inc., to have ridden the depression without resorting to bankruptcy, receivership, or reorganization of any kind. It has not even changed hands, and Harry, backed by Brother Abe and Brother Jack, is still in both managerial and financial control. The ride has left Harry with a nervous stomach, which keeps him at times on a light diet. Moreover, he is in no position to pay dividends on his 3,800,000 shares of common stock, which received their last cash payment in 1930 and will have to wait until $2,000,000 in arrearage is paid to the holders of the preferred. But his 1937 operations ending on August 28 showed a profit of just under $6,000,000...

Waddill Catching describes the movies as a rat-in-the-corner industry. Developed late, its laws are rat eat rat. Under these laws, the Warners have fought their way to the top against the opposition of the whole amusement world, which involves almost everybody from AT &T to Bette Davis. The fight has left its mark on the brothers. They have not yet lowered their guard. They are neither in Hollywood nor of it.

The huge 135-acre studio at Burbank operates somewhat like a moated feudal city, from which raids have occasionally been conducted against their more easygoing competitors, but which has not often been raided from without. Their production methods, in many respects unique, are mostly self-developed. Their personnel turnover is small. The Warner Brothers trust few people outside their own camp, but in each other they have the most implicit confidence. "The Warner brothers personally," as Harry once put it, "have always construed themselves as one."

There were originally six Warner Brothers, but only four to keep in mind. Beginning with the oldest, they are Harry, who is something of a martinet; Albert (Abe), massive, genial, and bumbling; Sam, who is dead; and Jack, who lives in Hollywood and wears dishrag sport shirts in the Hollywood manner.

When Waddill Catchings met the Warner boys in December 1924, they were selling their pictures through franchise holders – powerful independent distributors who also advanced them some of the money to make their pictures, but not enough. "Most of our time, complained Harry to Catchings, was spent in obtaining money from loan sharks. It cost us as much as 40 per cent interest."

Even in those days the Warners were conspicuous for the reverence in which they held their budgets: **School Days** cost $50,000, **Why Girls Leave Home** $33,000, and both grossed around half a million. Impressed by this and by the frugal private lives that Harry forced the brothers to lead, Catchings took them in hand and raised some real money for them. With $800,000 of it they bought the Vitagraph Co., which had a nationwide system of exchanges and enabled them to free themselves from the franchise holders. By 1928 they were a $16,000,000 corporation. Within two years they were to be a $230,000,000 corporation. There has never been anything quite like that, even in the movie industry.

Sam had persuaded Harry to listen to a device that the Bell Laboratories had invented and that the more respectable studios had already listened to and nixed. Sam had conducted the work that made the device practicable-quieting the kliegs and the camera, and adapting the synchronizing technique to studio conditions. In this work Sam got help from the telephone company engineers. What Harry got from the telephone company, however, was something else again.

The original deal between the Warners and the telephone people made the Vitaphone Corp. (which Warner Bros. controlled) the exclusive licensing agency for their talkie patents. It was on this basis that the Warners sank some $800,000 in development work. But Harry and his brothers were really fighting from a corner. They had practically no money, there were no theatres equipped for sound pictures, the General Electric soundon-film patents were a menace, and finally there was John Edward Otterson, who had just been placed at the head of Electrical

Research Products (ERPI), the new commercial inventions department of Western Electric is of course A.T.&T's manufacturing subsidiary.

Otterson, the extremely Nordic ex-navy man whose later career at Paramount was described in Fortune last March, took one look at the Vitaphone deal, decided that it was inferior, and began to dicker directly with the big-timers like Jesse Lasky. Harry was also trying to lure his rivals into sharing the development costs of Vitaphone, though without any thought of sacrificing control. But all the big studios (except Fox, which had some patents of its own) felt or hoped that talking pictures were nonsense and refused to participate. They even signed an agreement not to exhibit any in their theatres until 1928. Meanwhile Harry and Catchings were also trying to interest General Electric in making Vitaphone its exclusive licensing agent too, but without success. As deal after deal fell through, Harry and Otterson were forced, with the greatest mutual reluctance, to go on doing business with each other or not at all.

Harry now began to find on every side a new reason to feel persecuted. Under the exclusive contract he was committed to buying 2,400 complete theater equipment from ERPI. While Harry tried to sell this apparatus to the theatres against the opposition of the big studio-owned chains and was having to carry such independents as were willing to install it, he was not only berated by Otterson for under exploiting but hounded for full payments by the tenth of every month. Moreover, the price of the various parts, which had not been set in the contract, turned out to be about five times as much as he had expected to pay. It is scarcely to be marveled at that Harry couldn't sell as much equipment as the telephone people thought could be sold.

As for the Big Five, Harry does not blame them now for resisting sound, but he is sure they wanted him to go broke. As for ERPI, it was sorry, but this undercapitalized "upstart" was just not cut out for the job.

In April 1927, Otterson served notice to the company that he was through selling exclusively to Vitaphone. He and Catchings negotiated a new contract, by which Vitaphone gave up its exclusive rights but was also relieved from its crushing purchasing commitments. Vitaphone also was to receive 37.5 per cent of all royalties received by ERPI from other licensees. Having lost over a million in 1926, Warner Bros., which now owned Vitaphone 100 percent, began to make a little money. And when *The Jazz Singer*, which cost $500,000 to produce, began its historic climb and grossed $2,500,000, Otterson began to sell sound equipment as fast as he could make it.

The demand was so great, indeed, that the royalty he had promised Vitaphone was exactly 8 per cent of each licensee's gross that was traceable to the license. The telephone company was making a long manufacturer's profit anyway. Otterson moved to fix the royalty at a flat $500 a reel without Vitaphone's consent. Whereupon the Warners, charging breach of contract, took their case against Otterson before arbitrators. The telephone company settled in 1934 for $4,000,000 cash. But the Warners were by then not dependent on the ERPI patents. They now use R.C.A.

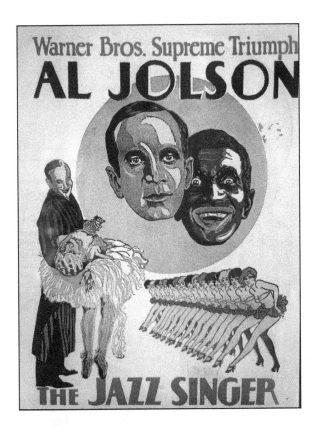

When *The Jazz Singer* sent his persecutors yapping on a new scent, Harry knew he could not hold his lead for long. As soon as the big-timers could make enough talkies to supply their chains, Warner Bros. would be just another independent producer once more. To forestall this, in one furious burst of family pride and financial sorcery, Harry became overnight one of the big-timers himself.

Harry's buying spree, which lasted from 1928 through 1930, ran Warner's gross assets up to $230,000,000 was conducted with less cash than confidence. Without the stock market he would have had less of both.

Harry Warner, the hero of this story, may not be so witty as his brother Jack, but he is more surprising and his career is more entertaining than some of Jack's movies. Warner Bros. reached the top so suddenly that Harry's real stature as a businessman is only beginning to be truly assessed. His stockholders had to sue him in order to find out that he had been their best friend.

Back in 1926, when Barrymore's **Don Juan** was shown with a musical score, Warner Bros. (somewhat reluctantly) had learned a play from Catchings that was to stand the company in good stead more than once. That was to sell their personal holdings and lend the proceeds to the company. It was these loans, amounting to $5,000,000 in 1928 that enabled Vitaphone to survive its early persecutions.

In 1928 Bryan Foy, directing shorts in Hollywood, happened to spin a two-reel talking melodrama called *The Lights of New York* into five-reels, and thus made the first "all talking" feature. The total cost was $21,000. It did a $75,000 business in a single week at the Strand in New York and ultimately grossed about $1,000,000.

That spring the Big Five gave in and wired their studios and chains for sound. On the strength of these phenomena and various merger rumors that summer, Warner Bros. stock went from 39 to 139 a share. And on the strength of that phenomenon, Catchings actually swung the merger that put Warner Bros. once and for all on its financial feet.

That was the acquisition of the Stanley Co. of America, which controlled some 250 theatres and also owned a third of First National Pictures, a first-class studio and whose producing reputation made Warner Bros. look like celluloid butchers. With cash from the banks and from sales of his stock Harry bought out the scattered holders of another batch of First National for $4,000,000. Later he acquired the final third from William Fox for $10,000,000. He also bought enough new theatres to run his chain up to more than 500 houses.

During the first half of 1930 he was averaging better than one new theatre a day. He bought Witmark, Remick, Harms, and other music publishers. For its patents, its record factory, and its stillborn sixteen-millimeter home talkie projector, he bought the radio, record, and phonograph divisions of the Brunswick-Balke-Cellender Co. and lost $8,000,000 on the deal. He bought radio companies, foreign sound patents, and lithograph company. He produced *Fifty Million Frenchmen* and other Broadway shows. He raided Paramount and bought Kay Francis, William Powell, and Ruth Chatterton with contracts whose generosity was limited only by their agents' imaginations. He shot the works. *Variety* dedicated an entire issue to the Warner brothers. They had arrived.

Harry Warner is a small, strong, swarthy man of fifty-six with a deceptive cupid-bow mouth and a vague resemblance to George Arliss. Willful and a worrier, constantly preoccupied with his own thoughts, he often fits that Hollywood definition of a producer: a man who asks you a question, and gives you the answer. He has two major interests: business and morals. In lighter moments these take the form of speculation on the price of a billiard table Paul Muni gave him or of heavy epigrams on how to handle women. Having worked himself since he was eight years old, he is in despair at the indolence and lack of initiative he beholds around him since the new labor movement. "Hard work never hurt me," he says; "on the contrary it developed me very fine."

An iron will, and a non-money-making father, he has been the head of the house of Warner since its earliest days. That responsibility has relaxed a little, as he is now merely the court of appeals, or trouble department. Harry Warner is still the undisputed boss of Warner Bros.

There are two things to remember about Harry Warner. One is that he is very shrewd, and the other that he is very proud. Unless you remember both, you might think there was something fishy about the details of his company's career. This is the mistake that various stockholders made when they launched a series of suits, asking for receivership, charging fraud, nepotism, and mismanagement, and demanding payment for 90,000 shares of stock that the brothers had been voted to do at their stockholders' meeting of 1928.

The brothers did turn back more than half this stock during the suits, but on all counts they were vindicated in the U.S. district court in Delaware last spring.

Now the Warner boys have had a family holding corporation called Renraw, which has served a double purpose. Primarily, it was a symbol of their family solidarity, owning the personal services of the brothers. Until a few years ago Harry did not permit the brothers to accumulate individual fortunes. Their joint salary which was $100,000 a year, until The Depression set in, was paid to Renraw, and each took what he needed to live on and no more.

Lewis

Harry had an only son, Lewis, precocious, hard-working, and idolized by his father. Renraw was so drawn up that on the death of the brothers, Lewis would automatically have become its head. But Lewis died in 1931, in his twenty-third year. That was the end of a good part of what Harry calls his "dream." It was also the beginning of the end of Renraw as a family stock. Harry was learning anyway that you cannot completely control two married men, however fraternal; so to avoid family trouble the money was split three ways. But Renraw had another use.

This was to act as a sort of 6 per cent Santa Claus toward Warner

Bros. Pictures Inc, whenever that hard-pressed company could not raise cash anywhere else. At one time Harry hocked his home and insurance policies to supply his cash. But after 1926, Renraw was generally pretty well heeled, for a very simple reason. That reason was the flaming condition of the stock market. When the brothers originally incorporated the business, they got 300,000 of the 350,000 shares of capital stock issued. Throughout the development of sound, Renraw periodically sold this stock on the curb for cash, in accordance with the company's needs and a policy that Catchings called "turning a fire hose on the market." Renraw would then lend its money to Warner Bros. without security at current banking rates or less. In 1928 the brothers were down to their last 60,000 shares of stock and had advanced the company some $5,000,000, having also personally endorsed $5,600,000 of its other borrowings. After the Stanley deal, Warner Bros. got $16,000,000 from a public issue of stock position to regain its own stock position and entered the year 1930 with over 300,000 shares.

Catchings resigned from Goldman Sachs in 1930 and the firm abruptly pulled in its horns. When Harry returned from Europe that summer, he found that Warner Bros. had some $16,000,000 in bank loans, which contrary to his expectations, Goldman Sachs did not then want to refund in a new stock issue. Harry had even expected to refund some $40,000,000 of debentures into common. But in the face of these debts, the market being high, Renraw had gone to work again. It sold stock from February to June to the amount of $16,500,000, or enough to cover the bank loans. Then Hayden Stone, batting for Goldman, Sachs, floated in August a $15,000,000 issue of new stock, so that Warner Bros. was able to pay off the banks without Renraw's help. Renraw therefore turned around and bought back 325,000 shares of Warner Bros. common for $7,500,000, the market having gone into the tail spin that ultimately took Warner Bros. to fifty cents a share. Renraw thus ended 1930 with more stock than it started with and its cost was $9,000,000 less. Had Warner Bros. not been threatened with the need of cash, Renraw never would have sold. The Santa Claus business was very good that year.

The movie business, however, got rapidly worse. As theatre receipts dropped nearly half their length, Harry's $106,000,000 of funded debt looked more and more mountainous.

Other chains were going into receivership, and to Renraw, which owned a lot of debentures, it seemed a tempting way out for Warner Bros.

But Harry, remember, is proud. He would never have been happy with a safe fortune drawn from the backward spelling of his name—"Renraw" backwards is "Warner." Besides, he and his brothers had all that common stock. Accordingly, he gave his brothers a lecture on the family honor and they all went to work.

If show business had forgotten that the Warners could be tightwads, it learned it again now with a vengeance. Running expenses of the theatres were cut by $123,000 a week. Marquee barkers were made to buy their own Listerine; and landlords, under pressure from a roving band of Warner negotiators were induced to cut rents and mortgage interest. Executives and errand boys took cuts; Joe E. Brown's name was sold to Quaker Oats; even the high-priced contract stars took a 50 per cent cut for eight weeks, although the stars had Zanuck on their side resisting it and he made it his ostensible reason for quitting. By 1931 the brothers resumed their role as the company's backstage angel.

Their timely loans have assisted the company in buying up leases and other obligations and in the remorseless lopping of no less than $31,00,000 from the funded debt. Renraw itself is no longer active, nor have the brothers sold any of their holdings since 1930. They have, instead, bought up most of the preferred stock (which, having gone off dividend in 1932, now elects a majority of the Directors) and about $5,000,000 worth (face value) of debentures. With another $5,000,000 worth that they already owned, they and their families now hold a third of the total outstanding debentures. This frees them, as officers of Warner Bros. from undue apprehension about the refunding of the debentures that must soon take place. It also gives them, as individuals, a nice lien on Warner Bros., which their brave economies have brought back to a state of health.

Warner Bros.' gross consolidated income for the year ending last August was about $100,000,000. Probably $54,000,000 of this, and about half the company's $6,000,000 profit, came from its chain of 480 theatres. The operation of these theatres is controlled by a tough and closemouthed ex-Philadelphian named Joe Bernhard, who comes as near as any of Harry's executives to taking equal rank in the organization with Abe and Jack.

Warner Bros. originally acquired theatres to put itself on an equal distribution footing with its rivals – you buy my product and I'll buy yours. Concentrated in the populous East, the Warner theatres are even stronger tactically than numerically, besides being profitable. Bernhard, through this zone managers, oversees all operating details. But a large part of his job, curiously enough is to see that the latent bargaining strength of his chain is never exercised. He competes not only with other studios' chains but with main very jealous independents. If Bernhard and the Warner sales department were to act too tough in the same area at the same time, the Department of Justice would be only too quick to hear about it. Thus, Bernhard leans over backward to keep the sales department at arm's length, especially in view of what the company has already been through in court...

Most of Warner Bros.' other revenue—probably $40,000,000 last year—comes from film rentals exacted from its own and other people's theatres both here and abroad. Besides negative cost, this revenue must cover the cost of distribution, which is one department in which Harry seldom has to shoot trouble. It is headed by Abe, the second Warner, who, Harry once wrote Catchings was known as "honest Abe" and was "the most popular man in the movie industry." ("As for myself," Harry added, "I may be disliked by some of the big men.") Honest Abe, who is also treasurer of Warner Bros. is not so active in the sales end as he used to be, and he is now generally called "Major." The Major's title is genuine, having been given him by the army in return for Warner's propaganda pictures. Harry, who was out of town on that occasion, ordinarily represents the family when such honors are bestowed.

Warner Bros. makes sixty pictures a year on a budget of $25,000,000. Warner's budget is not the smallest in the industry, but it is the smallest per picture in relation to what the average Warner picture grosses. Of the 214 Warner pictures released from January, 1933 to the end of last year only one has not yet returned its negative and distribution cost, thus contributing to the corporate profit. This does not mean that they were good pictures. It means that they didn't cost very much to begin with and that every one of them hit its budget on the nose. That is a famous Jack Warner specialty.

To begin with, Jack's 135-acre lot in Burbank is in many respects the best-equipped studio in Hollywood. It is a maxim of Harry's (who likes to play handy man around the dovecots and chicken runs at his ranch) that a good workman's first need is good tools, and within the last two years he has spent about $3,000,000 improving the Burbank plant. The sound department alone, which, has been buying, making, inventing, and patenting new technical devices represents an investment of more than $1,000,000.

Most studios build their sets from scratch on the sound stages where they are to be shot. At Burbank the sets are preassembled by straight-line production methods in a huge open Crafts building in the middle of the lot. This releases the stages for more shooting time. It also keeps the carpenters and other building labor in plain view.

The very size and scope of the Warner lot, in fact, are merely means to a million small economies. Everything in creation is stored there so that practically nothing ever has to be bought.

But Jack's important savings come from the way he handles talents and ideas, which are the really expensive ingredients of a movie. Jack and Harry are almost the only showmen who agree with the starched-collar crowd and have put their belief in practice. Paramount, for example, operates more or less as a loose federation of powerful producers, each of whom runs amuck as his own temperament dictates. But at Burbank it is a point of dogma that the company is bigger than any individual.

Jack doesn't even call his men "producers" nor does he like to give them screen credit until recently. They were officially "supervisors," which in Hollywood is almost a term of abuse. For creative men in so close an atmosphere, these supervisors are a surprisingly contented lot.

Supervisor Lou Edelman's specialty is the headlines, which also give him ready-made plots. "Anything worth newspaper space is worth a picture," he says, and keeps a scrapbook full of current clippings from six daily papers. The Warner story department seldom has to buy anything.

A still more spectacular corner cutter is Bryan Foy, whom we met about as the director of *The Lights of New York*. Foy learned to respect the dollar by being brought up in vaudeville (his father was Eddie Foy), and later became a shoestring independent producer of the most opportunistic stripe. Foy, in short, heads up all Jack's "B pictures," as he hates to hear them called, and thus guards the real backlog of the whole Warner program.

Jack Warner, Joe E. Brown, Hal Wallis

Such, in brief, are a few of the men who make Jack's pictures for him. Over them all, under Jack, sits Hal Wallis, who used to be the studio publicity man and is now called "Associate Executive in Charge of Production." Wallis initiates many scripts and passes on all of them, dickers with stars, assigns budgets, and in fact takes bows for the whole Warner picture program, excepting "Foy's B's." Things are so smoothly organized at Burbank that when Jack is in Europe (where he goes annually to see the shows and returns with so many antiques that his Beverley Hills home is nicknamed "San Simeonette"), Wallis can run the studio without him. There are also, of course, the twenty-odd directors, among them a few top-notchers like William Dieterle, Michael Curtiz, and Lloyd Bacon; but none of them is permitted to do anything more than follow the script.

Nor is anyone permitted to make retakes at Warner Bros. unless the preview is extraordinarily sour. At M-G-M they scarcely start work on a picture until after the preview, but in Burbank, where Jack or Wallis sees all rushes daily and retakes are made the next day. A picture whose shooting schedule is over is definitely "in the can."

The dispatch with which Warner Brothers go through the mill is in one way counted a blessing by the actors. They are not much coached or argued with because their time is expensive, and they consequently have more freedom to act. In Dick Powell, Pat O'Brien, Joan Blondell, Glenda Farrell, George Brent, Kay Francis, and others Jack has assembled a sort of permanent stock company who fall efficiently into each new role with an easy feeling that they have seen it before and will get home for dinner. But when he gets hold of a star with the authentic influence, Jack is likely to have more than his share of trouble. He had most with Cagney, who got sick of being typed as a girl-hitting mick and of making five pictures a year instead of four. He expressed his dissatisfaction in such way as growing a moustache, talking to Jack in obscene Yiddish, and finally suing his way out of his contract on a technical breach of a billing clause. Jack is still after him in the courts.

The Bette Davis case was somewhat more pathetic. In the hope of adding a few lengths to her reputation by taking to the law in England. She paid most of her fortune to get beaten, and is now back at the old grind under Jack, who has exchanged with her profuse expressions of forgiveness.

Now Jack's bargain-counter dictatorship has produced some excellent pictures, as we have noted. If he does not allow much liberty of temperament on his lot, he is very far from discouraging liberty of imagination. But there is one man there who enjoys both. Mervyn LeRoy a small and jumpy man of thirty-seven who look younger and smokes gigantic cigars, is Harry Warner's son-in-law. Before he married Doris Warner, in the presence of a Vitaphone camera and a microphone at the Waldorf-Astoria in 1934, he had won a reputation as Hollywood's boy-genius by directing **Gold Diggers of 1933, I am a Fugitive of a Chain Gang**, and others. Le Roy is on excellent terms with Harry, but his producing reputation owes nothing to the kinship, and he is recurrently rumored to be on the point of leaving Warner for another studio. He has one of the two private bungalows on the Warner lot. Mervyn Le Roy produces what he wants to, makes his own budgets, and shares the profit on his pictures, which are very good pictures indeed and often have unhappy endings. One of them was **They Won't Forget**, which is the most honest dramatization of a social problem that has lately come from Hollywood. Le Roy, however, is genuinely distressed at the resentment this picture has aroused in Georgia. He made it because Doris, whose story judgment he respects, thought it was a punchy script. He himself is prouder of having made **Tugboat Annie**. Very far from being a moralist, he was counted on to add professional finish to the Warner product, but not necessarily for any regular supply of Pentecostal thrills. Jack's humbler laborers such as Lou Edelman, up to his waist in headlines and propaganda, are just as likely to keep audiences alive to social issues as is Mervyn Le Roy. Likelier still, however, is Harry.

Harry who lives in Mount Vernon, New York has recently been spending more time in California, where he owns a beach house in Santa Monica, formerly Jesse Lasky's. He has also recently built himself a simple ranch house in the valley north of Hollywood. He is still landscaping the ranch and part of this job consists in removing three large hills that partly block his view of the mountains beyond. Watching the tractors at work, he says, "I stand here and bewilder myself at the amount of dirt they have moved." Harry has an almost mystical feeling about the land, which he associates with hard work and the salvation of the soul. He takes a lot of kidding at the studio for his mountain moving, but he envisions his ranch as a flat saucer terraced with fruit trees, and he will go to any expense to make it so, intending that the trees bearing shall remind his heirs that the land is their true source of strength.

Harry has a profound urge to stamp his feelings on the world as well as on his family. He says now that it was the educational possibilities that first attracted him to talking pictures; he is working on an ambitious program of school room films; and he has issued a series of commercial shorts on American heroes that he will rent free to anyone who can assemble an audience. The one on Patrick Henry, **Give Me Liberty** he would rather watch than any other Warner picture, but he believes that all the Warner pictures contain some moral lesson. "The motion picture," he says simply, "presents right and wrong, as the Bible does. By showing both right and wrong we teach the right."

Although he can relapse with startling suddenness from this plain to the details of a real estate deal, there is no reason to doubt the genuineness of Harry's messianism. It has two bases. One is his own lack of schooling; the other is his violent hatred of all forms of human prejudice and persecution.

Harry is so violently anti-Nazi that his incalculable influence could be all too quickly enlisted in America if the democratic nations should go to war. But in time of peace, if you see Harry's proselytizing hand in a movie, it will be raised against the injustices that he has to feel and hopes you will not have. And when, as is usually the case, his pictures pretend to be nothing more than entertainment, you may be sure you are getting a lot for his money.

Harry Speaking at American Legion

Tribute to the American Legion Speech

By Harry Warner
SEPTEMBER 19, 1938

"I thank God every night that such an organization as the American Legion exists in our country. Alert to the ever-present danger to our institutions and methods both from within and without the borders of this nation, the American Legion has become the watch dog of democracy—the guardian of equal rights for all. Warning to destructive interests the world over that Americans will stand, if necessary, in support of true democratic government and against the hates and prejudices of a world gone mad.

In recent years, since various foreign governments have fallen into the bloody hands of dictators, autocrats, and tyrants, other organizations have grown up within our own borders. These groups are inspired, financed and managed by foreign interests, which are supplying a new never-ending stream of poisonous propaganda aimed directly and indirectly at the destruction of our national life.

These organizations stand as a constant threat to the American Legion because they seek to take your place and usurp your rights and powers to the end that our country may become a terror-ridden copy of their unhappy lands. But only the American Legion can be the bulwark of true Americanism from which men and women like you must go forth each week, each day, each hour, to combat these unwelcomed, un-American forces. Those who seek to change our system of government and to sow the seeds of discontent, of intolerance, and national destruction, are our common enemies and we can never relax in our vigilance against them if America is to fulfill her splendid destiny.

The fundamentals of Americanism were established long ago. A group of truly inspired men, determined to establish a haven for the oppressed people of the earth, wrote into the Constitution a Bill of Rights which has no equal anywhere on earth. All the hopes and prayers of man and women who had been victims of oppressive governments too long were incorporated into that remarkable document.

It has served as the backbone of our great nation for more than a hundred and fifty years. It always will serve as long as you and I and all of us guard it against encroachment. I hope the necessity never arises but we know now that every true American must be eternally on guard and ready to make the necessary sacrifices if sacred duty calls.

We stand, as always, dedicated to the cardinal principles of liberty and justice for all and we have been trying in our humble way to contribute to the welfare and peace of our country through the pictures we make here.

You may have heard that Communism is rampant in Hollywood. I tell you this industry has no sympathy with Communism, Nazism or any 'ism' other than Americanism. We collectively and as individual studios are doing much – all we can do in fact – to teach the principles of true democracy to the outside world. I defy our accusers to prove that this industry is run by 'isms.'

Certain bigots representing the malcontents who want to ruin what they cannot rule, and whisper that Hollywood is run by 'isms.'

They lie! They lie when they say it. Let them show us the slightest proof of their cheap accusations.

Here in Hollywood we keep faith with American ideals because, like you, we believe in them, because they have brought peace and happiness to us when nearly all the rest of the world is miserable and afraid.

We bring to the talking screen patriotic shorts and historical subjects dealing with the high spots of American history and showing the firm foundations upon which our government was built. We tell the outside world every day the true principles of our great democracy. The world knows that ours is the best-advertised nation on earth and I believe that motion pictures have played the most important part in making it so. We will continue to tell the world how worthy while it is to be American, working and living under American government, enjoying the freedom of thought, freedom of worship and life guaranteed by the American flag.

The world looks upon America as the strong frontier of democracy because the motion picture has given them a true conception of our institutions and our life here. People the world over believe that America is the greatest land of liberty and the textbook from which they have absorbed that lesson has been the motion picture.

Within the industry I am known as a man who calls a spade a spade. I tell you Catholic, Protestant, Jew, or whatever faith you observe, that we must all be Americans first, last, and always. Don't just say you are an American. Act like an American. Be Proud of America!

If this flag is waving I, for one, am proud of it. We need more flag waving. We need a renewed consciousness of our national life, of the blessings we enjoy under our flag, of the security we feel in our homes and offices because that flag floats, figuratively or actually, above everything.

The American Legion is the backbone of our patriotic enthusiasm. It is visible evidence that we value our heritage and intend to keep it intact. Its deeper significance will not be misunderstood or misinterpreted by foreign dictators or despots who turn envious eyes toward our shores or send sneaking emissaries into our institutions, hoping to bring this nation to their own sad state of decay.

Drive them out. Make America unsafe for those who seek to tear down what others have built up through the generations since 1776. Drive them from their secret meeting places; destroy their insidious Bunds and their leagues, their clans and Black Legions, the Silver Shirts, the Black Shirts, and the Dirty Shirts. Help keep America for those who believe in America. I repeat. We must be proud of being Americans proud of the American Legion and all it means and will continue to mean throughout this and future generations.

As one who holds very dear the rights and privileges it has preserved for us and for the liberties it will continue to guard, I say: 'God bless the American Legion!' I will not forget."

"I do hope that we will continue, and in the course of time as I can see it before me, the world will be a better place to live in than it is at present. So let us live in the future, and radio and talking pictures hand in hand will develop to a point where dreams of others may come true." –Harry Warner

---

Hollywood's Obligations As a Producer Sees Them

Harry M. Warner
Christian Science Monitor
MARCH 16, 1939

"It is the producer's attitude that usually determines the content of any picture and the strength of his faith in the ultimate good judgment of the majority will be the guiding factor in keeping the Hollywood product worthy.

The men and women who make a nation's entertainment have obligations above and beyond their primary commercial objective, which is the box office. In the long run Hollywood, collectively, and producing companies individually will succeed or fail in my opinion, exactly in the proportion in which they recognize these obligations.

The problems of production, distribution and exhibition of motion pictures are many and varied. But with the mechanism of our industry fairly well established, we can give earnest consideration to our implied duties to ethics, patriotism and the fundamental rights of individuals.

The motion picture producer shares this obligation with the schools, the churches, the service organizations of all kinds of which stand for tolerance decent thinking and fair relations with the rest of mankind. I do not mean that we should attempt in the theater, to teach all the lessons, preach all the sermons or solve all the political problems of the world.

We cannot do this, but we can and should give a helping hand to the causes of good government and of fair play. The motion picture can be a great power for peace and good will or, if we shirk our obvious duty, it can stand idly by and let the world go to pot. I think we are making an honest effort to use the screen's influence for the greatest general good of humanity. I am proud that my own company has had some part in this.

Hollywood believes in America as firmly as any community or any business believes in it, and we possess the added advantage of being able to express our faith in the common language of the screen.

A motion picture involves a large sum of money and a great amount of effort on the part of many people. Several thousand artists, artisans, laborers and specialists have a hand in every production and each and every one of them tries his best to make a good picture.

I feel that America is putting its best foot forward in the world of nations because the Hollywood-made motion picture has given other peoples a reasonably true picture of America, extolling the values of its Democratic principles and the advantages of living where personal liberties have not been curtailed.

There is an ever-present duty to educate, to stimulate and demonstrate the fundamentals of free government, free speech, religious tolerance, freedom of the press, freedom of assembly and the greatest possible happiness for the greatest possible number. To that end our company and, I believe, our whole industry stands pledged—now and for the future.

As long as there are varying tastes, different viewpoints, incompatible interests in the world; we as producers, must seek to please the greatest possible number of future patrons. We believe we owe that to our audiences our stockholders and ourselves.

The success of a picture is measurable not only in dollars and cents returned but in the worth of the principles it illustrates. All producers feel that they have a duty to the nation as well as to the industry to help keep uppermost in the public's mind the advantages we all enjoy in this country.

The screen should attempt to explain the why and wherefore of the current struggle and not repeat on a formula proved profitable. There are forces in this land who would like people to live in darkness. I take issue. It is the people who are fighting this war – and it is the people who must be given every opportunity to examine each why and wherefore."

"The 'human' type of picture appeals to every
person in every walk of life." –Harry Warner

Harry Warner at Saint Patrick's Day
Dinner-dance at The Royal Palm Hotel

MARCH 17, 1939

"I am here as an American. We are friends, brothers, sisters, Americans all. But I have my own personal conception of St. Patrick. To me he has always seemed one of the kindliest of human men. A genial man, not an austere, aloof man. A man whose heart overflowed with love for his fellow men. A man to whom you might go and offer your hand, and have that hand accepted. A smiling, good-humored man with tenderness in his soul and friendliness in his eyes. A man who won your love and kept your love, because he wanted you to be his friend, and he wanted to be your friend.

It is pretty well agreed, I think that between the Jews and the Irish in our own beloved country there has long been a bond of friendship and goodwill. I will not say that this is because your people and my people have both suffered persecution, although that as you know, is the case. Perhaps it is because our peoples are imaginative peoples, aggressive people, and ever-hopeful peoples.

The first important step in the preservation and defense of Americanism, it seems to me, is to exalt Americanism—to be proud of being an American. Show these Un-American individuals and organizations that you are watching them, that you know their true purposes, and that you do not intend to permit these purposes to be carried out.

We are tolerant, yes. We have a constitution and a Bill of Rights that given to everyone—to naturalized citizens as well as to the native-born – the privilege of assembly, of free speech, of free beliefs, civic as well as religious. But I often wonder if we are not too tolerant.

Our Producing Company is making right now a picture revealing the astonishing lengths to which Nazi spies-have gone in America. We are making this and we will make more like it, no doubt, when the occasion arises. We have disregarded threats and pleas intended to dissuade us from this purpose. We have defied and will continue to defy, any elements that may try to turn us from our loyal and sincere purpose of serving America.

Here Harry Warner discusses the importance of Haym Solomon and the new film being released by Warner Brothers about him. Haym Solomon (1740-1785) was a Polish Jew who immigrated to New York during the period of the American Revolution, and who became a prime financier of the American side during the American Revolutionary War against Great Britain.

Harry Warner at the Dinner of the Patriotic Foundation of Chicago

MAY 21, 1939

Naturally we, like everyone else in business, are not prone to losing money. But our studio sincerely believes that it has a duty, in fact, many duties to our nation. We have made many patriotic short subjects and we are now gratified to offer the story of Haym Solomon.

This picture, just like our other patriotic shorts is available for any school church, or American organization without cost. We of the Warner studio are sincere in our desire to impress upon the American youth of today the real truths about our beloved country.

You men and women of Chicago are to be congratulated on your great "I Will" spirit in carrying through to completion the first memorial to honor three great men of our Revolution: General George Washington, Robert Morris, and Haym Solomon."

"It's high time for a few more American moviemakers to awake to the fact that pictures are more than young romance entertainment. They are universal textbooks in philosophy..." –Harry Warner

---

Letter to President Roosevelt from Harry Warner

MAY 20, 1940

"Because of criticism by some who do not recognize the terrible potentialities of the present European situation, I have hesitated to communicate with you in recent months.

But now in the wake of the news that barbarism continues to advance to unfortunate peaceful nations, destroying innocent women and children, we are too deeply concerned to remain silent. The brave people who are fighting, giving their lives for the cause to insure future peace for us as well, as for themselves, may need not only our moral but material help.

Here in Hollywood we are worried for fear the so-called "cash and carry" system will work too great a hardship on these brave, unfortunate nations who are, in a way, fighting our battle for us. The least we can do, it seems, is to supply all the material help we can command, short of actual troops and so help destroy the barbarian gang that is overrunning the world today.

Personally, we would like to do all in our power within the Motion Picture Industry and by use of the talking screen, to show the American people the worthiness of the cause for which the Free Peoples of Europe are making such tremendous sacrifices. We cannot stand by and watch others die for the civilization, which is ours as much as theirs without taking some part in the struggle.

I have been very ill for the past year and under the advice of my doctors have had to take things a little easier than in past years. Still I cannot contentedly sit still out here and do nothing while the whole world echoes with the march of the savages out to destroy all any of us holds dear. I would rather die in an effort to be helpful than live to see barbarism triumph."

"My mother and father did not come here to earn a living, they left everything behind so their children could have a home in a place where everybody has an opportunity." –Harry Warner

---

Speech by Harry M. Warner

EARLY 1940S

"The motion picture industry would be shamefully remiss if it were not now looking ahead to its task in the post war world. The essence of the task can be stated in a single phrase: 'To interpret the American way.'

I have a right to speak for my own company only, of course. We at Warner Bros. have sought for more than a decade to combine entertainment and point of view. We have tried to say on the screen the things about America and democracy and Fascism that needed to be said. If we have pioneered in that field, we do not mean to detract from the other producers who also understand that motion pictures have a higher duty to perform even than press or radio.

The screen transcends language, time, distance, and custom. It stands on no protocol, requires no artificial Esperanto to make itself understood. Through the screen, millions of Chinese, Icelanders, Indians, Eskimos, Russians, to name a mere handful of races, know how Americans live and what Americans stand for. One of our chief aims now in the post-war world will be to show Americans how millions of Chinese, Icelanders, Indians, Eskimos, and Russians live. I can think of no clearer, surer way to achieve a community of nations; and certainly no clearer, surer way to show the world what our democracy means."

Speech by Harry M. Warner

JUNE 5, 1940

Public calamity is a mighty leveler. Bursting shells and exploding bombs from the skies and machine gun bullets are no respecters of race, color, or creed.

I have talked to the highest and lowest, and each in turn said to me, 'Why, nobody would dare to invade us. No one would dare to attack us. What would they want with us?'

I am not so much worried about the enemy from without. I am worried about the enemy from within.

This company, therefore, is of as much interest to you as it is to me, and I know you all take it that way. I know that in walking around I meet those who have been here a long time, and no greater pleasure do I have than when I see the same faces.

I have a great deal of faith and confidence in the future of mankind. I cannot for the sake of me, for one moment think that everybody in this world is no good.

Calamities have taken place in the past. History tells us that. Attilla the Hun existed and he was destroyed. Oppressors have been destroyed in the past; they will be destroyed in the future. And I am sure that we who have faith, whatever that faith may be, will in the long run survive in a greater world hereafter.

It is only when we are aloof from one another that we get to hate each other. When we can sit around and discuss what is on our minds, that's the time we can do something.

I know that every one of you has been taught the words of Christ. Where can you find anything finer than 'Peace on Earth, Good Will to all men.' He didn't say, 'Peace on earth and good will to any particular faith.'

When the first persecution took place in Germany against a people that have a faith, the mistake that the civilized world made was that it did not rise against any people who attack any minority because they have a faith. If that had happened, I would not be standing here today pleading with you that you should protect your children and their children, so that they may continue to have a faith.

As I see it, we have a very simple problem here and that is: 'United we survive and divided we fall.' We must unite and quit listening to anybody discussing whether you or I am a Jew or a Catholic or a Protestant or of any other faith, and not allow anyone to say anything against anybody's faith or we will fall just the same as they did over there, because we are confronted with the greatest organized machine, subversive or otherwise, that the world has ever had. And what bothers me is how we can have supposedly sane-thinking Americans who consciously or unconsciously are playing into the hands of dictators and helping to divide us. I would think that if we know that the man who is coming into the second story window is going to kill either ourselves or one of our family that we would try to defend ourselves. This is no different from anybody coming into any part of our country and using all of these methods to divide and destroy us.

Everybody, knows, there is no secret about it, that our Company does not make any profit from our patriotic shorts, but we keep on making them.

I say this to our people and to our investors: the cheapest investment they can make is to allow us to make these pictures even though they lose money, because if we don't succeed in destroying the enemies of civilized people, no matter what we have won't be worth anything.

The first two hundred thousand of these pamphlets, describing our Patriotic Shorts are going into schools and the pictures are being shown in schools. Authorities have finally come to take them seriously. They have come to appreciate that these patriotic shorts, depicting the glorious background and traditions of our country and honoring men who have fought and died that this nation might live, have struck a responsive chord in the hearts of our people.

We don't want any bundsters, Communists, Fascists, or members of any other unAmerican group in this studio."

"The film *Sergeant York* is a factual portrayal of the life of one of the great heroes of the last war. If that is propaganda, we plead guilty. So it is with each and every one of our pictures dealing with the world situation or with the national defense. These pictures were carefully prepared on the basis of factual happenings and they were not twisted to serve any ulterior purpose..." –Harry Warner

---

Harry Warner Testimony at Senate Interstate Sub-committee Hearing to Testify Concerning Alleged Propaganda in Motion Pictures

FEB. 24, 1941

"I am opposed to Nazism. I abhor and detest every principle and practice of the Nazi movement. To me, Nazism typifies the very opposite of the kind of life every decent man, woman and child wants to live. I believe Nazism is a world revolution whose ultimate objective is to destroy our democracy, wipe out all religion and enslave our people just as Germany has destroyed and enslaved Poland, Belgium, Holland, France, and all the other countries. I am ready to give myself and all my personal resources to aid in the defeat of the Nazi menace to the American people.

I realize that my convictions are of themselves unimportant. However, I am proud of them. As a matter of fact, I have never made a secret of them. I have always believed that every citizen has the right to express his views. I have done so both among my friends and associates and publicly to the press. I stand on my public record of the last eight years. But for the record of the hearing and to avoid misinterpretation, I should like to summarize my convictions. They are not newly found convictions. They are deeprooted.

While I am opposed to Nazism, I deny that the pictures produced by my company are propaganda, as it is alleged. Senator Nye has said that our picture *Sergeant York*, is designed to create war hysteria. Senator Clark has added *Confessions of a Nazi Spy* to the isolationist blacklist. John T. Flynn, in turn has added *Underground*. These witnesses have not seen these pictures, so I cannot imagine how they can judge them. On the other hand, millions of average citizens have paid to see these pictures. They have wide popularity and have been profitable to our company. In short, these pictures have been judged by the public and the judgment has been favorable.

Sergeant York is a factual portrayal of the life of one of the great heroes of the last war. If that is propaganda, we plead guilty. *Confessions of a Nazi Spy* is a factual portrayal of a Nazi spy ring that actually operated in New York. If that is propaganda, we plead guilty.

So is it with each and every one of our pictures dealing with the world situation or with the national defense. These pictures were carefully prepared on the basis of factual happenings and they were not twisted to serve any ulterior purpose.

In truth, the only sin of which Warner Bros. is guilty is that of accurately recording on the screen the world as it is, or as it has been. Unfortunately, we cannot change the facts in the world today. If the committee will permit, we will present witnesses to show that these pictures are true to life. I am certain that we can easily prove to you that Warner Bros. has not duped its patrons but has, in fact, kept its obligation to the movie-going public.

Apparently, our accusers desire that we change our policy of picturing accurately world affairs and the national defense program. This Warner Bros. will never do. This, I am sure the Congress would not want us to do. This, I am certain the public would not tolerate.

As I have said, reckless and unfounded charges have been made before your committee against Warner Bros. and myself. These charges are so vague frankly, I have great difficulty in answering them. However, they have been widely disseminated and maybe believed by the uninformed. I have tried to summarize the charges. They seem to divide into four allegations.

1. That Warner Bros. is producing a type of picture relating to world affairs and national defense for the purpose of allegedly inciting our country to war.

This, we deny. Warner Bros. has been producing pictures on current affairs for over twenty years and our present policies are not different than before there was a Hitler menace.

2. That Warner Bros. pictures concerning world affairs and national defense are inaccurate and are twisted for ulterior purposes.

This, we deny. The pictures complained of are accurate. They were all carefully researched. They show the world as it is.

3. That Warner Bros. is producing pictures that the public does not wish to see and will not patronize. The proof of the pudding is in the eating. All of the productions complained of have been profitable. To the point is *Sergeant York*, which, I believe will gross more money for our company than any other picture we have made in recent years.

4. That, in some mysterious way, the government orders us to make this or that type of picture.

This, we deny. We receive no orders, no suggestions – direct or indirect – from the administration. It is true that Warner Bros. has tried to cooperate with the national defense program. It is true that Warner Bros. over a period of eight years has made feature pictures concerning our Army, Navy, and Air Force. It is true that we have made a series of shorts portraying the lives of American heroes. To do this, we needed no urging from the government and we would be ashamed if the government would have to make such a request of us. We have produced these pictures voluntarily and proudly...When we showed our first picture, thirty-five years ago, we wanted to please, entertain and inform our fellow-townsmen. Today that is the objective of our studio, on a national scale.

In order that I may show how prejudiced and misinformed are the charges against us, I would like your indulgence again to explain in some detail how Warner Bros. operated. I as president of the company wish to assume the full responsibility for the pictures we produce. That is a responsibility that should be mine, and one from which I do not shirk. However, I would not be telling you the truth if I left you with the impression that I personally select or supervise the pictures that we make. To be successful, a motion picture company must utilize the skilled men both in the selection and production of pictures. I would never be qualified for such an intricate and delicate job.

Our company has been successful, I believe, because we have recognized that motion picture production cannot be dependent upon the feelings, intuition or knowledge of any one person. Instead, we have assembled the best talent available. Their job is to select from the huge amount of material that is presented to us, the subject and stories in which they think the public would be interested. Their job is to present it on the screen in a way that will attract and please the public.

I have the idea that our accusers believe that I, together with one or two others, sit down in secret conference and plot the kind of pictures, which we propose to make. Nothing could be further from the fact. Our success does not depend upon my personal opinions, it depends upon millions of Americans who find entertainment and enjoyment in pictures.

This then, is the cardinal principle of Warner Bros., to produce motion pictures of all kinds, with the one objective of giving to our customers a wide variety of the kind of entertainment they want.

But again, I want to be frank with this committee. As I have indicated, our company has pioneered what, for a better phrase, I will call "an action picture." By that I mean, we have tried to portray on the screen current happenings of our times. We have tried to do this realistically and accurately and over a long period we have discovered that the public is interested in and grateful for this type of picture. Perhaps I can explain what I mean better by listing a few of these pictures.

We produced *British Agent*, which was an expose of Communistic Russia based upon the book by Bruce Lockhart. We produced *Black*

Fury, which was a factual portrayal of conditions in the coal mining industry. We also produced many realistic biographies of such great figures as **The Story of Louis Pasteur**, **Juarez**, **Dr. Ehrlich's Magic Bullet**, and **The Life of Emile Zola**, who aroused the conscience of the world in behalf of Dreyfus, the victim of religious bigotry.

I have no apology to make to the committee for the fact that for many years Warner Bros. has been attempting to record history in the making. We discovered early in our career that our patrons wanted to see accurate stories of the world in which they lived. I know that I have shown to the satisfaction of the impartial observer that Warner Bros., long before there was Nazi Germany, had been making pictures on topical subjects. It was only natural, therefore, with the new political movement, however horrible it may be, that we should make some pictures concerning the Nazis. It was equally logical that we should produce motion pictures concerning national defense.

If Warner Bros. had produced no pictures, concerning the Nazi-movement our public would have had good reason to criticize. We would have been living in a dream world.

Today, 70 percent of the nonfiction books published deal with the Nazi menace. Today, 10 percent of the novels are anti-Nazi in theme. Today, 10 percent of all material submitted to us for consideration is anti-Nazi in character. Today, the newspapers and radio devote a good portion of their facilities to describing Nazism. Today, there is a war involving all hemispheres except our own and touching the lives of all of us.

I am an American citizen, and I bow to no one in my patriotism and devotion to my country. Our country has become great because it is in truth, a land of freedom. No one can take these freedoms from the American people. The United States has always been a united nation of free people living in tolerance and faith in each other. We have been able to achieve this unity because of the freedoms of the individual.

I tell this committee honestly, I care nothing for any temporary advantage or profit that may be offered to my company or me. I will not censor the dramatization of the works of reputable and well-informed writers to conceal from the American people what is happening in the world. Freedom of speech, freedom of religion, and freedom of enterprise cannot be bought at the price of other people's rights. I believe the American people have a right to know the truth. You may correctly charge me with being anti-Nazi. But no one can charge me with being anti-American."

"It is said that a universal language would solve many
of the problems of maintaining peace. Well, motion
pictures come as close to being a universal language as
we are likely to get in our time." –Harry Warner

A Statement to the Employees of Warner Bros. Pictures, Inc.

Delivered by its President, Harry M. Warner
Warner Bros. International News Bureau
MARCH 27, 1942

One hundred feet of wasted film may cost the life of an American soldier who may be your own son or brother. I am not asking you to eliminate waste merely because of its dollar and cents value, but because of the materials involved. It makes no difference if you're in the picture business or the grocery business. Every foot of lumber, every nail and every bit of material is vital to the war of production that our country is waging with our enemies. It is this all out marshalling of our resources that is going to prove the decisive factor in this struggle for freedom. Therefore, it is up to every individual to save, save and save on materials to forge into munitions, ships, guns, tanks and planes.

One sheet of paper wasted may appear insignificant. But, unfortunately, there may be 130 million sheets of paper wasted in a single day throughout the United States. Think of what that means in terms of machinery tied up and labor employed that could be utilized for war production.

A take is ruined because a mike shadow was cast upon the face of a player or the player missed his lines. It is just a hundred feet or so of wasted film. The dollar value is trivial, but the material value is great. For just multiply the wasted takes throughout the industry, and we having a staggering total of film material lost. Once again, the manpower and material and machinery needed to replace that waste could be freed for war production.

Who would have thought just a few months ago that tin cans would be so important in the film business? Yet, unless we can return empty film cans we can't get any new film because of the shortage of tin for our war machinery.

We have not as yet, and when I say "we" I mean the American people, gotten down to an all-out war effort. It isn't enough that we buy defense bonds, act as air raid wardens, help in civilian defense or our sons go off to fight. It is up to every single man, woman and child to start thinking and practicing wartime economy at home and in business. And that doesn't mean merely the saving of dollars. It means the saving of our nation's resources, the conversion of materials and the absolute elimination of waste.

We in the motion picture business use tremendous amounts of materials of every description. Materials that today are of vital importance in our national defense. Let us, by our almost fanatical devotion to the elimination of waste, make free this saving of materials for war purpose.

Waste is criminal at all times but in times of war it is worse than the sabotage of enemy agents. After all, saboteurs can destroy only so much, but with 130 million people daily wasting materials, the aggregate loss is staggering. And conversely, the saving can be enormous. Therefore, I again urge everyone to help America win this war by constant vigilance against waste.

"Never before has Hollywood been producing such good pictures as today. These excellent productions are raising the cultural standard of the entire world." –Harry Warner

---

Plea Renewed for Red Cross at Rally Here

FEBRUARY 14, 1942

This statement was given by Harry Warner concerning a blood drive held by the Red Cross to support the soldiers now going off to war, post Pearl Harbor. He is encouraging people to donate money because the Red Cross was struggling to reach its fundraising goal.

'Will the cry be here, as it has been after each depressing defeat of our gallant allies,' 'Always too late, always too little!'

We at home have an obligation to support with all our efforts and all our resources the heroic men in uniform and the millions more soon to be in uniform at the fighting fronts.

I am shocked at the indifference of too great a portion of the American people in this crisis. Think of it, the American Red Cross, which is a definite and vital part of American's national defense, finds its drives lagging in this, one of the richest communities in the land!

Warner Brother Number One "No More Stunts"

FREDERICK VAN RYN
Liberty Magazine
DECEMBER 12, 1942

"Nothing is stronger than human resistance to accepting knowledge. Nothing is weaker than people's ability to distinguish between diamonds and glass."

The former conviction was expressed by Theodore Roosevelt. The following observation was made by Harry M. Warner.

A consummate politician, Mr. Roosevelt understood that a successful vote getter must sugar coat the unpalatable truth. A showman extraordinary, Mr. Warner realized that a successful producer must out-Barnum P.T. Barnum and make Baron Munchausen look like George Washington.

There is a lot in common between the election campaigns of the first Roosevelt and the promotion campaigns of Harry Warner, but nothing at all in common between the publicity methods introduced by the Warner Bros. and those used by their predecessors.

Young Harry

When Harry managed to elbow his way into the industry about 1918, publicity was still considered notoriety. The ballyhoo racket (it was a racket) was controlled by a handful of Broadway press agents. They made money, plenty of it, but they delivered little. Every blessed promotion relied on his ability to outwit the newspaper editors and befuddle the public, none possessed real tools or developed anything resembling a technique.

Harry Reichenbach (the number one press agent of that time) would bring a gorilla into a Broadway hotel, that being his way of hinting to the denizens of New York that they were about to behold a Tarzan picture.

Will Page (another ace of the period) would overhear a wrenchingly beautiful Ziegfeld blonde say, "I'd rather eat with a pig than with that horrible fat man," and bingo! Page would immediately throw a party at which the outspoken young lady would be seated next to—yes, you guessed it – a real pig.

Still another luminary would hire 300 young unemployables, put them in dinner jackets, and order them to walk in and out of a certain

Broadway picture house, thus creating the impression that the place was patronized by Society.

As stunts go, those were not bad, but unfortunately for the future of the racket, they were overtaxing both the patience of the editors and the credulity of the public.

The episode made an everlasting impression on Harry. He saw the handwriting on the wall. It became clear to him that promotion men must either change their methods drastically and immediately or face sudden death.

"No more stunts," he ordered his publicity department. "From now on, I insist on legitimate news."

There was, of course, and still is a slight difference between "news" as the editors of the New York Times understand that word and "news" as the Warner Bros. grasp it. The venerable New York paper does not create news, it merely covers the news. The Warner brothers, on the other hand, feel it is their duty to lend a helping hand to unborn events. Unlike the New York Times, they create news—legitimate news, to be sure.

In the past ten years the Warner brothers grabbed more free space in the newspapers than all the other motion picture companies combined. Favoritism? Not at all. It's just that editors do not throw legitimate news in the wastepaper basket. One may laugh off the story of a gorilla lunching at the Astor Grill, but even the most hard-boiled managing editor in America must give space to a dispatch dealing with the arrival of six trainloads of celebrities at Dodge City Kansas. What if that dispatch should mention also that all those governors, senators, federal judges, movie stars, and opera prima donnas made the pilgrimage for the express purpose of witnessing the world premiere of *Dodge City*, a Warner Bros. picture starring Ann Sheridan. What of it, indeed! The point remains that six special trains, coming from the east, south, north and west did reach Dodge City.

The knack for turning a so-so picture into legitimate news and smash hits with the aid of a junket was developed by the Warners in 1933. In the month of February of that tragic year when the banks were dying and the motion picture business was so bad that even the Broadway houses were playing to empty benches, the brothers had a brainstorm. "Bank holiday or no bank holiday," they decided, "people still want to be thrilled. They'll appreciate a good laugh now more than ever, provided we tickle them in the right fashion." It must be explained that at that moment they had on their hands a picture known as **42nd Street**, a musical which had set them back a million dollars and which was certain to lose at least half of that sum because of the panic.

Harry visualized a train, a long glittering train made up of pullman cars and carrying a huge electric sign in the rear which read "*The 42ⁿᵈ Street Special.*" He put himself in the position of a person living in a small town situated somewhere between Los Angeles and New York.

Suppose he were to pick up his morning newspaper and discover that *The 42ⁿᵈ Street Special*, with numerous Hollywood stars aboard, would arrive at the depot and remain there for three hours the following day. Would he be tempted to take a look at the stars? The odds were five to one that he would. More than that, not only would he go to the depot, but when a week later he noticed passing by his neighborhood playhouse a sign reading **42ⁿᵈ Street**, he would rush in, because having seen the stars, he would want to watch them act.

The success of *The 42ⁿᵈ Street Special* is history. Exhibitors still speak of it in hushed tones. Wherever the train stopped—it seems to have stopped at almost every railroad station in the United States—it left a wave of prosperity in its wake. The other theaters benefited as well. "Things can't be so bad as we thought," said the customers, "if a hard-boiled motion picture company was willing to spend a fortune on a crazy stunt like that."

In the eight years that followed the brothers conducted many more junkets. Thanks to them and their desire to create legitimate news, several hundred American newspapermen, not to mention governors, senators and federal judges, were given a chance to see America on the cuff. Preparedness is the motto of the Warners.

Once upon a time, acting with the best intentions in the world, they asked their guest of honor, the governor of a southwestern state, to appear on the platform of the observation car and make a short speech. The governor was obliged, but the reaction of the crowd filled the hearts of the brothers with anguish. Instead of giving a big hand to the man who was introduced as "that outstanding American, that great executive, that peerless statesman," some 2,000 men and women yelled, "To hell with him, we came to see Gene Autry and his horse."

Pearl Harbor and America's entry into the war put an end to junkets. Nowadays, the Warners spend money not on creating legitimate news but on making numberless shorts that popularize the deeds of American heroes, the technique and routine of flying, etc.

A pioneer in the field of anti-Nazi films (he broke off relations with the Axis way back in the 1930s,) Harry Warner insists that, at least for the duration, each and every picture that comes out of the plant at Burbank should be more than mere entertainment. He outbid all other companies on the movie rights to Irving Berlin's *This the Army* because the author and all others responsible for the show have agreed to turn the profits over to Army Relief.

His favorite time of day is that hour which he spends at the luncheon table in the executive dining room. Not because of the food but because of the conversation. An orator and debater, he thrives on cross-examining people. No subject—be it mechanized warfare, the shortage of scrap, or the newest ways of using sulfa drugs— stumps him. An "expert" invited to partake of food at his table usually feels as if, instead of loafing in the glamorous atmosphere of a motion picture studio, he had gone through a whole afternoon of merciless grilling.

At a recent Los Angeles banquet, which was to usher in a charity drive, Harry was introduced as "the outstanding success of our times." He smiled, got up, and studied the master of ceremonies as if to make sure that he was not kidding, then said:

"Ladies and Gentlemen. So, I'm supposed to be a success—an outstanding success at that. Well, let me tell you of a talk I had not so long ago with my doctor. I wasn't feeling too well. I thought I'd better go and see him. First of all, he asked me whether or not I did any drinking. I replied honestly that once a month, I did take an occasional cocktail or high ball. 'Stop it,' he ordered. Then he looked at my cigar and said, 'I see you smoke cigars. How many a day?' "Oh, three or four, doctor." 'Stop it at once. No more smoking for you. And now, what do you eat?' I confessed that I ate what most people eat. Chops, and chicken and steaks. 'Aha,' he said. 'Chops and chicken and steaks! We'll see to that. I'll give you a diet, and there won't be any chops, or chicken or steaks on it.' So, here I am, ladies and gentlemen. I can't drink, I can't smoke and I can't even eat what I like. But I'm a success."

> "Writers, directors, and technicians are the ones to whom the real credit for good productions belongs. Never before has Hollywood been producing such good pictures as today. These excellent productions are raising the cultural standard of the entire world..." –Harry Warner

Speech by Harry M. Warner; Warner Bros. Studio; Weekly Variety Annual

JANUARY 6, 1943

"It is being said, with considerable solemnity but much rooted in truth, that the duty of the motion picture industry 'in these days,' is dual and clear: it must entertain and inform.

The whole truth is that in the minds of most persons 'these days' mean the 'war days,' whereas any thinking individual recognizes that the first days of peace will be as critical and bewildering as the most grievous day of the war period. Actually, the early days of the peace may well be more confusing to the average citizen, since there will be more subtlety and justice required that come during the mass clashing of whole armies.

In the hot conflict of warring national ambitions, a sensible man can take his stand for liberality and humanity and with that stand can work to see to it that the only acceptable side wins. He may don a uniform and fight for it direct, or he may remain a civilian and do his apportioned share by war work at home, by denying himself for the good of his army, by pledging his resources to the maintenance of his country at war. In the time of actual war, hysteria and emotion are much a part of the individual and he must not only discipline his own thought but receive from cogent sources all the guidance possible.

When the peace comes, the necessity for guided thought and informed opinion becomes even more acute, lest the now quieted forces impose on a weary world an even more terrible and destructive condition than that of full war.

In the hands of motion picture makers lies a gigantic obligation. No one man, humble before the fierce winds sweeping his world, can look upon this responsibility with anything but awe. It is at once an honorable responsibility and a frightening one. In the very nature of motion picture creation such a man must somehow, somewhere find the wisdom to coincide his responsibilities now with a condition which may obtain months ahead. The mechanics of creating a photoplay are slow and no good way of speeding them up yet has been found. Thus, a filmmaker today may think of an informative subject pertinent to its hour, only to find six months later that his finished product is sadly out of step with the swiftly changing times.

Wisdom, the fullest possible information, a precise weighing of the probabilities and let us admit it, an injection of luck, all help a man or a studio, earnestly trying to stand before an appalled world to say, 'In this way and to our uttermost we have tried to fulfill our duty.' For myself, I am proud of what my company, under the productive direction of my brother, Jack L. Warner, and his associates, has done and is doing.

Long ago, when the crooked cross of Germany first appeared on a horizon in turmoil, we sat down all of us together and mapped a course. At the same time, we pledged ourselves, no matter what history and fate brought to us, to carry out this course. I believe, and with pride, that up to this point we have done so and that we will continue to do so.

The responsibility to entertain and inform implies much more than a photographic mirroring of the times. It implies an understanding of and harnessing to the intangibles. These intangibles are best illustrated pictorially. A mighty truth was uttered by a Chinese philosopher when he said that "one picture is worth a thousand words."

However skilled the press and literature have been and are in their reporting of the war, however sincere and faithful radio has been, I must still hold that the motion picture is the perfect reportorial form for a world in a state of uproot and violent change. Before a screen, humanity may sit and watch the other parts of humanity as they play their roles in this monster conversion. We may sit in our theaters and with our eyes look upon the Poles, the Greeks, the English, the Chinese, Russians, the French, and the Africans as they live day by day and meet the problems of the hour.

Nor does this needful visual examination of the transforming world take a citizen away from his grave duties to his country at war. Indeed, people do not have too much time to read these days. More's the pity. A man should read, he should read all he can lay his hands on that makes sense, but war work, war duties, and war events prevent planned study reading and contemplation. And that is precisely where the motion picture meets with destiny and obligation. In a motion picture theater, in less than two hours, a person today can inform himself, can start preparing his thinking for the future and, while this critically needed information is coming to him in the fastest, clearest way possible, he also is being entertained.

In our own way, my brothers, myself, our producers, writers, directors, players, labor, skilled technicians, all as one, started facing the issues and history years ago.

We are all telling stories of today and of the days to come. These are stories of how we live, how all of mankind lives. How man is living and working to win his terrible fight for the rights to exist free and clean upright. They are the fruit of these times.

And I like to think that to some appreciable degree these pictures have given escape and entertainment in dark times, also have given counsel and wisdom to meet the history, yet we do not know the shape of the peace, but since we are to meet these, let us meet them in an informed way."

"Its central and all-important theme is democracy, and there is no need for me to point out how vital to the world is the necessity of keeping alive the still-surviving democracies, beginning of course, with our own United States of America. Intense patriotism is the most valuable asset a democracy can have. As picture-makers we have tried, and will continue to try, to inspire patriotism by means of the screen." – on the film *Juarez* –*Harry Warner*

Making of War Pix a Duty to Public, Says H.M. Warner

The Hollywood Reporter
MAY 20, 1943

"When the war is over, Warner Bros. does not want to be known as the company that made the greatest musical movie during the war.

We will leave the fairy tale version of the world we live in to that small group of entertainment appeasers which is presently at work in this industry or being pressured by groups from the outside. It is this group which refuses to recognize that the American motion picture audience has an adult mind.

Even the younger element is far more intelligent than it is given credit for being. Boys of 18 are now going to war. That means the 16-year-olds already are thinking seriously of what's ahead for them. They want to know what they are going to fight for and about, and the screen must help to make the issues understandable to them. If we don't do this we are failing our most important obligation.

I wouldn't believe it, not for a single moment, if someone were to tell me that any mother who has a son with the victorious American forces in Africa, can't wait for dinner to be finished so she can rush to her radio and hear ANYTHING BUT the latest news.

And I can see no reason to believe that the same mother goes to the neighborhood theatre these terribly trying days in order to flee any mention of this war in which she and her son are so desperately involved.

No, the mother, father, sister, brother, sweetheart, friends and neighbors of the man at the front are not anxious to run away from anything. They want to know the truth. They want to know what their boy is doing, and how he's doing it, and most important, WHY he's doing it.

Americans are not fighting this war simply because they have remembered Pearl Harbor. We are not spending these precious lives and breaking up these treasured homes to satisfy merely 'just for revenge.' I like to think-in fact, I know, that this great worldwide struggle is being endured for something as specific as a universal guarantee of the Four Freedoms. The measures by which we will obtain this new and greater democracy and the significance to each and every one of us of these freedoms must be understood.

Here is where we of the film industry come in. With a medium reaching forth to the greatest mass audience in the world, we have an obligation and duty far more vital than the mere smiling away of two hours on a dull mid-week evening. People want to be entertained, but not nearly as much as some might think.

Leisure hours are scarce and win-the-war Americans learned long ago that the value of an hour is doubled when it is employed to collect entertainment and information simultaneously. There are forces in this land who would like the people to live in darkness. I take issue with them. It is the people who are fighting this war. and it is the people who must be given every opportunity to examine each why and wherefore. If it has been our good fortune to be among the pilots of an industry capable of presenting information and understanding in the most palatable form yet devised, then let us steer a proper course.

Were we to do anything else at such a moment, when so many are making great sacrifices, there would be no point for our existence.

We must work to eliminate shortcomings and catchpenny tricks or having a cheap superficial attractiveness designed to encourage quick sales.

Let us NOT make a war picture just like several other war pictures simply because the others proved profitable. There are many facets to this war, a large part of them requiring delicate handling and considerable courage on the part of the man who would attempt to picturize them. This, then, is our chance to demonstrate that we possess that necessary courage and sensitivity, and our chance to make all other Americans feel damned glad that we were numbered among them in this crisis.

So, let's pay heed to the apologists among us. We have a vital role to play in this drama and an awaiting audience that is literally starving for brain food. Those who would ration it are those who have always looked down from their isolated ivory towers and sneered, 'Ah what does the public know?' Well, we here say the public knows a great deal more, and who will stand in their way?

Remember this—Ignorance never won any kind of fight and there is little reason to believe that timidity will help it win this one.

And to the exhibitors of the country I want to say, don't be intimidated or coerced by persons who are not whole-heartedly behind our war effort; don't be influenced by those who are trying to keep the truth from our audiences.

The exhibitor's responsibility to his community is bigger than it ever has been. He is one the most important bulwarks of the home front. Like the newspaper and radio, he must do his part in keeping the public informed as well as entertained. Any arbitrary exclusion of war films, either to satisfy a small appeaser element or for personal reasons without regard to the general public interest, is equivalent to sabotage.

A radio station wouldn't think of barring war news and programs. A newspaper certainly wouldn't put a ban on dispatches from the fighting fronts. And the motion picture theatres of the country likewise cannot ignore the things that are foremost in the public mind.

I don't believe there is an exhibitor anywhere who wants to shirk his duty. I know every single one of them wants to be right there in the front line doing his utmost to help bring an early end to this war. Without this cooperation from the exhibitors, we cannot have the strong united home front that we need to back up the boys at the battlefront.

In the years to come, the contributions of our industry to the winning of the war will be tabulated and appraised. By what we are doing now, we will be judged in the future."

"The world looks upon America as the strong frontier of democracy because the motion picture has given them a true conception of our institutions and our life here." –Harry Warner

---

Harry Warner Speech to Safety Committee on the Warner Lot

American Jewish Archives
Harry Warner Collection Reel #407
1943

"What I am going to talk to you about tonight is a little off the beaten path, however, I want this kept within the studio as it is no one's business outside of the studio. I ask you to please remember this. Each of you get the man near to you and talk to them along the lines I am going to talk to you. This concerns you and your families as well, so please take it seriously.

I would like to take my time with this talk, but unfortunately, I am little nervous. Not what I am going to talk you about, but about some other things. There is a condition that exists in the world today that neither you nor I are responsible for. There are wars going on all over the world. Neither you or I or this company created them, on the contrary, we did a great deal to try and prevent war.

A great thing happened just today, when a decision was handed down in Supreme Court, written by Judge Black, when four Negroes, who were sentenced to die, were given a new trial. No matter what color or creed a man may be, we have a law and a Constitution to live up to and no man should be made to confess to something he didn't do. 'Therein lies our future,' said Judge Black.

There are things happening in the studio, which I do not like. Literature is being distributed right in the studio. I have checked very carefully and find that one of the men in the Carpenter's union is responsible. I can't say who this particular carpenter is but I do want to impress you with the fact that the men who work around you are very, very important to you, because one man can cause the ruination of a great many.

I have had reports about certain things which have been going on around the lot, and I might add here, that what I want to I find out. I don't want to hurt anyone, but I do want you to understand how much harm one bad man can do to this plant, including you. You men who protect a man of this type are even worse than he is because you know that he is destroying you and your families and you aren't doing anything to stop him.

The greatest excuse the majority use is to say, 'He is a Jew.' Thank the Lord, I was born from a father and mother whose name I am proud to bear. I never ask anyone whether they are a Jew or a Christian, as this isn't important. The Lord never spoke any greater words than, 'PEACE ON EARTH, AND GOOD WILL TOWARDS MEN.' It doesn't matter of what faith a man is, but does that man have a faith? This is no place to discuss whether a man is a Jew, a Christian, a Catholic, a Protestant, or whatever faith he may be.

You should get all of your men together and tell them that we must get rid of the troublemakers.

I am personally not interested, if it weren't for the fact that this business supported some 20,000 people, I would quit. I don't have to work. It is only for your benefit I'm working every day. I assure you I have sat around more hours than I care to mention, thinking how I could help Christianity.

I have been working for days on a story called, **The Miracle** our next big picture. It is the story of one who left their Christian faith, and after trying everything else, found that real faith is in Christianity. So, I am interested in only one subject—that day when people come back to Christianity.

Somehow or other a report has come to me regarding a subject about which I am more vulnerable than anyone else. I can't deny that Mr. Dies now says that this studio is communistic. He might just as well have said that Shirley Temple is communistic. I must admit that we made **Confessions of a Nazi Spy**, but Mr. Dies particularly states that *Juarez* is communistic. I won't go into the question with the man. I would be a damn fool if I answered him. The best thing to do is keep quiet. My father, rest his soul in peace, always said that when you get into a problem where the other man wants what you are seeking, keep quiet.

I don't have any objections to anyone finding fault with my work, I even welcome them to come in and discuss it with me.

You should see the correspondence I have received from various people complaining about their Community Chest subscriptions. What I am trying to do is educate them. There are 42 men in our business who make seven and a half million dollars a year, and don't give a damn nickel. There are 180 men who draw eighteen and a half million, who only gave $13,000.00 to the Community Chest. By God, if it is the last act of this Jew's life, they are going to give, or the public is going to know about it. I mean business. I am not going to fail.

Remember, we have offices all over the world, all run by very fine men. There is Mr. Kaufman, who is a German, and he ran our office there. However, one night an officer walked into his home at 1 o'clock in the morning, knocked him down and kicked him, and he died six months later. There was not reason in the world for them to do this to him except that they thought he was a Jew. When, in fact, he was a British subject born of German parents."

"America was carved out of the wilderness by initiative
– an initiative forged in lonely pioneer fires and
tempered on the expanding hearths of industry. As
long as it remains our heritage there can be no closed
frontiers in all the Western World." –Harry Warner

Speech by Harry Warner to the American People
Regarding Motion Pictures in the Post War Period

JUNE 20, 1944

"Each year more and more people come to realize the importance of the motion picture in our way of life. As the realization grows, something else grows with it. That is the ever-increasing responsibility of picture makers and exhibitors to make and to show pictures, which in the long run will be regarded by the public as a force for good in the land.

That is why we made *The Adventures of Mark Twain*. We wanted to bring to the screen in these difficult times the life of a great American whose story would remind us of the great heritage of our country. *Mark Twain* proves that a picture can be an influence for good without sacrificing any commercial benefits.

The motion picture is such a force to an extent never dreamed of in times past. It is such a force merely by virtue of the numbers of people it reaches and the fascination it holds for them.

I believe that whether we like it or not our pictures have a profound effect on people who see them. Whether a producer makes a picture for pleasure or for profit; for pure entertainment or for pure education or just for art's sake, he's up against the incontrovertible fact that his picture will produce some effect, for good or bad, on its audience.

As businessmen, we try to make pictures that will make money for our company and exhibitors.

As members of the entertainment industry, we try to make pictures that will provide pleasure and recreation for those who seek it.

As Americans, we try to make pictures which will be a force for good in our great country and which will advance public interest and welfare.

Motion Picture audiences in the postwar period will be the most enlightened of all time, and exhibitors not only must take this into account, but must strive as never before to combine their business operations with greater public service to help promote better citizenship.

We must do more than just keep the pace with the mental growth of the mass audience. We must be the ones to set the pace, always forging ahead, always providing new and better stimulants to broaden education. That is the way the motion picture industry can maintain its leadership as a social force working for the general good of mankind. And that is the best assurance of future progress and security for both producer and exhibitor."

Speech by Harry Warner

Bill Fullman's Theatrical Advertising and Publicity News
The New York Enquirer
DECEMBER 18, 1944

"For a long time, I have been interested in the problems of the returning serviceman. Long before it was required by law, our company promised that any bona-fide Warner employee returning from the armed forces could have his (or her) job back if he wanted it. We are sticking by that promise, but we want to do more than just give a veteran his job back.

I have always felt that proper readjustment of veterans to civilian life is the responsibility of every civilian, and this survey is one step, which our company has taken to meet the responsibility. We civilians are the ones who must go more than halfway to make whatever adjustment may be necessary. We owe that much to our service men and women. After all, they are the ones who have been doing the job that makes it possible for us at home to live in peace. It is their courage and sacrifice that makes it possible for us to have a free world for our children to grow up in."

Patriotism in Pictures Speech by Harry Warner

1945

"It is of equal importance to all and of great immediate importance to us, as showmen, charged with entertaining all that is left of the civilized world, to enjoy a Freedom of our own, The Fifth Freedom, as VARIETY calls it, the Freedom of Self Expression in All Show Business.

We have not sought to glorify war, we have only tried to honor our country and the men and women who stand ready, now as always, to defend it.

'In praise of liberty' as Variety so aptly puts it, Warner Bros. has long made pictures in which the proudest moments of our national story have been recounted and dramatized.

We hope we have helped build the idea in America that even in times of peace, patriotism is something of which we should be proud, which we should shout to the world as loudly and as often as we can.

No individual or profession has had or ever can have a corner on Patriotism. It is the inborn right of all Americans to be proud of their nation, and to say as much, by every means at their disposal. Here in Hollywood, and at the Warner Bros. studios, in particular, we have used our best means of communication—the motion picture screen-to tell the world of the pride we feel in the United States of America.

In motion picture production we follow no 'isms' except Americanism. We have fought, in our way, for the freedoms of thought, of the press and of speech and worship.

We were not the only voice, individual or collective, raised against the Nazi menace before we were actually at war. But the motion picture had to bear the brunt of much of the Senatorial displeasure during the recent, rather ridiculous effort to show that what we believe was good Americanism, was only propaganda in disguise.

Patriotism is not meant for one medium and poison for another. There is enough of it in America for us all to share! Motion Picture producers should not be denied their right to talk of liberty or seek a Fifth Freedom of their own.

The magnificent history of our country, the peoples' pride in our institutions, our form of government and our belief in liberty, have been and will continue to be reflected in the product we make in our studios…

What we have filmed has been the truth, not propaganda. and those who would curtail the freedom of our industry know it.

Certainly, **Sergeant York** truthfully can be called a 'Patriotic picture.' There can be no question of the patriotism of Alvin C. York. Neither can there be any doubt of the insight and good sense in his famous lines spoken in the picture as it was in life.

'You do not fight to win liberty and freedom and democracy once and then stop,' said Sergeant York. 'Liberty, freedom and democracy are prizes awarded only to those people who fight to win them and then keep fighting eternally to hold them.'

"Truth is not propaganda. Facts are not propaganda. The principles of democracy and the rights of man as expressed in our basic American documents are not propaganda."–Harry Warner

Ways in which the studio contributed to the war effort:

- 763 employees went to serve
- Employees bought $11,765,000 of the $20,000,000 war bonds the company sold
- 12 visits from the Red Cross resulted in the donation of 5,200 pints of blood
- 21 soldiers a day were given studio tours (31,365 total)
- In 10 years, 46 full-length pictures about the war effort and American ideals were made
- ***This is the Army*** raised $10,000,000 for Army Emergency Relief
- ***Hollywood Canteen*** raised $310,405 for the canteen fund

Harry Warner Speech at The American Nobel Anniversaries Dinner

DECEMBER 10, 1945

"It is a great pleasure and privilege to join with you tonight in honor of the memory of Alfred Nobel, and trying to find ways of making his dream of world peace a permanent reality. And I am glad that you recognize the possibilities of the motion picture as an instrument of world peace.

It is up to us to evaluate films in a positive as well as a negative way—to make use of film as a tool of international good will and understanding. For if motion pictures cannot give people a complete formula for making world peace permanent, they can still help create the conditions of international good will that are the essential foundation of lasting peace.

It is said that a universal language would solve many of the problems of maintaining peace. Well, motion pictures come as close to being a universal language as we are likely to get in our time. The question is, what shall we say in that language?

I think the motion pictures of one country can say to the peoples of other countries: 'We are human beings, just as you are. We laugh and we cry, just as you do. We love freedom, just as you do. We want to like you, and we want you to like us.'

Another thing motion pictures can do is to show the people of every nation how much their own welfare is dependent on the scientific, cultural and industrial achievements of other nations. Motion pictures can emphasize and dramatize the fundamentals of the world today.

The motion picture can accomplish these things only if it draws its inspiration from those fundamental human interests, which the peoples of the world have in common, rather than from the differences which tend to divide us into separate nations.

The problem of creating motion pictures that will be understandable to the people of less fortunate countries than ours is more difficult than it may seem. Take, for example, an American-made picture in which a family is destitute by American standards. In certain countries the audience will say, in honest bewilderment, 'How can these people be poor when they have electric lights in their home?'

Of course, the motion picture maker can't hope to solve the problem of different standards of living. But he can try to find a means of communication that will help to create a higher level of understanding for all men everywhere.

Whether the motion picture develops along these lines will depend largely on whether the motion pictures will be recognized by the nations of the world as a medium of communication to be accorded the utmost freedom of expression, or whether they will be treated as just another article of world commerce and subject to restrictions at every international boundary.

The danger is that under the pressure of economic urgency, governments will be blinded to the tremendous cultural importance of the motion picture. If we are sincerely interested in world peace, we should welcome every new ambassador of goodwill and every avenue of understanding.

If picture producers of all the nations are encouraged to think in terms of an international audience, we can look forward to the development of films, which will carry the spirit of one world to the far corners of the earth and interpret it so that men of all nations may see and understand.

I hope that the statesman of the world will see the wisdom of such a course in peace as they saw it in war. If they do not, the cause of world peace, and of humanity will be the loser.

And I think it is reasonable to say that any country which does not encourage the fullest use of the screen as a means of giving its own people a greater understanding of the meaning of peace on earth and good will toward men does not want peace on earth."

"Hunger and ignorance are the chief allies of totalitarianism. We must fight hunger with food and material aid. The Friendship Train was only a beginning but it proved the feeling and generosity of the American people." –Harry Warner

---

The Friendship Train Show

HARRY WARNER

1947

"Since the frontier days, when we were breaking open new lands, this tradition has been the simple act of holding out a hand to a neighbor. It was neighbor-helping neighbor that built the first cabins in the wilderness and brought in the first crops. Now, once again, neighbor must reach out to help neighbor from hunger.

Tonight, a train is leaving Los Angeles and will roll East across the nation. Americans will help load that train with wheat, flour, sugar and commodities that are desperately needed in the war-torn lands of our neighbors across the sea. There will be other commodities riding that train and that is hope and faith.

Here in California, and throughout our country, we are witnessing a wave of pride and generosity which stretched into every town and crossroads of the states. My own experience in working in this project has been one of the deepest humility. It was as though in preparing the timetable of The Friendship Train and in watching the new announcements coming in of carload after carload of food, I was seeing the history of America passed before my eyes, for it was in in the very shaping of this nation, that we learned the truth, that no man lives alone, that a peaceful world can come only out of the spirit of brotherhood and sacrifice. Here, in this rich and abundant land, we hold all the fruits of earth and what we do with them, will determine what kind of world our children will live in."

"The men and women who make a nation's entertainment have obligations above and beyond their primary commercial objective, which is the box office. In the long run, Hollywood collectively, and producing companies individually, will succeed or fail, in my opinion, exactly in the proportion in which they recognize these obligations." –Harry Warner

---

Back the Films Says Warner

New York World Telegram
MAY 26, 1948

"A theater in a community is a social unit designed to do the greatest good for all. There are things, which the motion picture theater can do and has done well to fulfill this community objective. Fund raising, morale building, dramatic presentation of vital information. These are motion picture activities aiming at the community objective for the greatest good."

Warner Urges Free Film Trade to Aid Relations

Motion Picture Herald
MAY 29, 1948

"The free and unfettered international distribution of American Motion Pictures would accomplish much toward the improvement of our relations with other countries," Harry M. Warner said Monday. The Warner Brothers President, speaking before the National Council for Community Improvement here in the capital said that, "Going to the movies has taught more than one person how to get along with the rest of the world. Wouldn't it be wonderful if we could show our pictures to Russia?

The motion picture and the motion picture theater occupy key spots in the progress of the community and through the community, of the entire country," he said.

"The greatest achievement of the motion picture in the community is that it has made history entertaining. It has given the American citizen more and more information from which he can make up his own mind. It has expressed, in terms of entertaining drama, the American ideas of tolerance."

Mr. Warner pointed out that although the primary function of the motion picture is entertainment it has so broadened the scope of entertainment that it has become a teacher.

The theater is the perfect headquarters for public service endeavors, because it attracts such great numbers of people, Mr. Warner explained. He cited as examples the campaigns for fire prevention, the conservation of fats and for periodic x-ray examinations to control tuberculosis.

The theater, "helps to knit the community together, serves as a spur to sound business on Main Street and fulfills a community need for a good recreation outlet."

Speech Made by Harry Warner in Los Angeles Regarding the Friendship Train

FEBRUARY 21, 1949

"During the darkest hours in our history, when we were fighting for our own liberty and independence, it was the people of France who came so nobly to our aid and helped us in the struggle, which led to birth of our own great America. It was the people of France who gave us our Statue of Liberty. Its lighted torch still stands as a beacon of hope for all freedom-loving peoples.

Our hands are clasped across the sea in an expression of brotherly love, which I hope and pray is the forerunner of peace on earth and goodwill towards all men among all the people of all the nations of the world."

Harry M. Warner's Acceptance Speech When Decorated with a Cross of an Officer of the French Legion of Honor

APRIL 7, 1949

"Thank you, Monsieur de Manziarly and the people of France. You will forgive me if I find it difficult to express in fitting words the feeling of humble gratitude that fills my heart at this moment. I can only tell you that in accepting this high honor from the gallant Republic of France I give my solemn pledge to strive always to be worthy of it and the noble ideals for which it stands.

Just a few weeks ago it was my never-to-be-forgotten privilege to participate with you in ceremonies welcoming The French Gratitude Train. At that time, I said and today I reaffirm, that nothing in my lifetime had so stirred me as that expression of thanks and affection from the great free people of France. I realized then, as never before, what friendship between free peoples really means. It is not something that can be bought sold or bartered. It cannot be destroyed by the stroke of a pen or the command of a dictator. It endures in the hearts of women and men and it is the one sure foundation for a world of peace and human brotherhood.

In all of history, the friendship between our two countries stands without parallel. Through 173 years of war and peace the people of France and the people of America have remained bound by the ties of friendship founded on the common precepts of liberty, equality, and brotherhood. Our hands always have been lifted together against foes of those precepts.

To have been able to serve France, as best I could, has been an honor and a privilege. To receive this Cross of an Officer of the Legion of

Honor is a distinction I shall cherish always. I accept it in all humility on behalf of the American people whose generosity and goodwill made The Friendship Train possible, and whose affection for France will never falter.

Trade Views

W.R. Wilkerson
The Hollywood Reporter
SEPTEMBER 5, 1950

Here Harry Warner in various quotes is speaking to his 2,000 Warner Brothers employees. He encourages them to fight against Communism.

"The Commies have made incredible efforts to infiltrate our industry and it would be stupid to argue that they made no converts. They did. They made converts here just as they did in every other industry in the United States. They subverted to their evil philosophy some people in Hollywood just as they did people in the fields of science, politics, communication, research, education etc. etc.

But they attack our industry the hardest because they know the power of our particular media of communication. The fact that they failed so miserably is proof of the solid foundation of Americanism on which our country is founded.

Don't be scared of anybody. Don't allow those bullies to bully you. You're good honest Americans. Why not stand up and fight."

More Thoughts on the Freedom Train
Declaration of Freedom Speech

SEPTEMBER 27, 1950

"Those who try to destroy, first destroy themselves. I undertook the job of The Freedom Train to bring to those French and Italian people something from the hearts of the American people.

Fear is the greatest evil.

I know Freedom and please bear this in mind, I know freedom by the opportunity that our country gave me. Not from the term of wealth, because, as my father also taught me, 'Wealth you can't take with you.' It is the things that I have been able to do for the good of all people. And today, I find, myself with eight grandchildren, and when I look at them it is a job to stand up under pressure looking at those children's faces and thinking, even thinking, the thought that they may not have a place on this earth where they can live except by slavery."

"The motion pictures are built of more than celluloid and scenery. Our industry, above any other, is founded on human values and is fostered by the idealism of the men and women in it." –Harry Warner

3,000 Hear HM Warner in Crusade for Freedom

The Manila Chronicle
NOVEMBER 20, 1950

"Grant us peace, Thy most precious gift. Bless our country that it may ever be a stronghold of peace and its advocate in the council of nations. May contentment reign within its borders, health and happiness within its homes. Strengthen the bonds of friendship and fellowship among all the inhabitants of the world. Proclaim Liberty throughout the land unto all the inhabitants thereof.

The Bible and the Bell are evidence of the inherent wish for freedom existing since history began. What we fought so hard to attain, we must fight still harder to retain. We must also aid those who cannot help themselves beyond the Iron Curtain by showing concrete evidence that we are their friends, that the lies they hear about our country are not true and that in fact the democratic way is the better way for human beings."

"It is said that a universal language would solve many of the problems of maintaining peace. Well, motion pictures come as close to being a universal language as we are likely to get in our time." –Harry Warner

Motion Picture Pioneer Awards

NOVEMBER 15, 1951
Speech by Harry Warner

"No award we have ever received has had the significance of the honor of being named 'Pioneers of the Year.' We are most grateful.

We want to thank the Motion Picture Pioneers, the trade press, the newspapers and all our friends who were so generous in their tributes.

In a large sense all of us engaged in so creative an industry as making of motion pictures are pioneers, and will continue to be pioneers as we continue to create new and ever higher standards of entertainment and public service for the millions upon millions who attend our motion picture theatres.

American enterprise has flourished because there are pioneers in motion pictures, in banking, in radio communications, autos and in other industries. In our industry, it seems to me, pioneer groups must dedicate themselves seriously to the broadest challenge we have ever faced. It is not the challenge of dollars. It is the challenge of ideas and ideals.

The capacity to earn a profit is very much a part of the whole American idea of free enterprise. But if we are to keep enterprise free, we must see to it that we keep ideas free, as well. The communication of ideas is as essential to our business as freedom of enterprise.

I don't presume to have any quick solution for the very serious problems of the world outside our industry. But I am concerned with the impact and effect of our business on the world itself. Motion pictures can have a tremendous effect both in this country and beyond our borders. They can portray the spirit and meaning of America in a way that nothing else can. But to do that we must seek and find the spirit within ourselves. The spirit of hope and vision. Having hope and vision is our job. Film is a public service.

If the producers of pictures see only the dollar sign at the end of their production efforts, then I believe those production efforts will fail. If distributors concern themselves with immediate technical problems only and do not realize that cans of film can distribute American ideals— they are failing in their job. If exhibitors concern themselves only with exhibition of film and forget that they have the responsibility of their leadership in their community—then they are guilty of wasted effort.

To you advertising and publicity men our biggest promotion now as always is to promote the response of the human heart to hope. Hope is the strength within us, because we know that in a country like ours anyone's hopes can someday come true.

It is what we do in the future that will affect the world. The potential force of motion pictures for good has just begun to be tapped. All we have done is only a foundation for future greatness, but we can take pride in the fact that our foundation is a firm one. It is solid bedrock for future generations of pioneers to build upon.

We are particularly pleased, when the plaque was presented to us as 'Pioneers of the Year,' to see engraved on it the words 'for unswerving faith in motion pictures and in their industry as a bulwark of the American way of life.'

This is the faith we held for half a century. With this faith we go forward confident as ever in the greatness of our industry's place in the world and more determined than ever, with God's help, to remain active in this industry.

We're here to help the human heart respond to hope and faith, no matter what their faith may be. I'm concerned with the impact and effect of our business on the world. Having hope and vision is our job. Film is a public service.

We wish to express gratitude to our co-workers and our exhibitor friends for helping us follow the path we have chosen. This is the industry to which we have devoted most of our lives. We look forward to long years together firm in the conviction that Warner Bros. Pictures always will hold a proud place in this industry's accomplishments."

Harry Warner Speech to Studio Heads

JULY 11, 1952

"My father also taught me when you stop looking, you quit living. I don't believe in the word 'can't!' I remember when I was a shoemaker and I told my father, 'I can't,' he hit me in the head with a shoe. He said, 'There is no such thing as "can't."' Say you'll try. I don't want to hear the word 'can't.'"

It's a great miracle to me that the world grows larger in spite of all the killings since Adam and Eve. Somebody must be doing something right.

I said to Mrs. Warner, 'Look, if I sell out, it has been my experience that of the men we bought out, no one lived more than five years. They all died before that. My dear, I doubt whether I could live a year, if I couldn't do the things I want to do.'"

The Hollywood Reporter Anniversary Edition

Harry Warner Speech
NOVEMBER 10, 1952

This is part of our destiny. It has been my privilege to see it spring from nothing. It gives me peace to know it will continue always.

To me, the motion picture always will be the most exciting thing that has happened in my lifetime. My brothers and I have been in the pictures since we were youngsters. It has been our privilege to have seen the steady growth in this magnificent business and to have helped build it. Not once during these many years, nearly the span of a man's life, have I failed to find excitement in the participation.

In medicine and the field of microscopic photography the motion picture has been a boon, adding substantially to the extension of man's life expectancy. New educational patterns have been opened up through the utilization of classroom films and sound projection.

The motion picture today is the greatest instrument for the enlightenment and education of mankind that the world has ever seen. From its inauspicious and shaky start in rented halls and corner nickelodeons, not even the wisest man could have foreseen its prominence in science, medicine, and research, even warfare.

Above and beyond these remarkable advances the motion picture has become a spokesman for democracy, carrying the message of brotherhood from this country to every corner of the world. During the black years that lay behind us it brought hope to a world where hopes had become fragile. In the bright years that, we pray to God, lie ahead it will exhibit democracy and unity of mankind to places where even the most persuasive statesman could not hold an audience.

But the most important part of the motion picture will play in the world picture will be in telling the story of the American way of life. This can and will be one of the most important weapons in combating the forces of ruthlessness and oppression, simply by showing America as the great country it is and Americans as happy, freedom-loving people that they are. In that way, without propaganda messages or oratory and by showing the simple facts of life here, the story of our country will hit home the hardest.

All of the way we have been in step with the growth of our country, expanding as it has expanded, spreading the influence of motion pictures over every country in the world and in some way to almost every person in the world. To have seen this and to have been a part of it is an honor. I can never forget filling me all the more with the sense of the duty we owe our country, our industry and ourselves.

And in our approach, we discovered that the lives of Americans, great or plain, tell the story of better than any fiction. Men of history and destiny, statesmen, frontiersmen, show people, song writers, doctors, soldiers and cowboy philosophers, their lives carry the unmistakable brand of the greatest country in the world. These pictures, playing in distant lands, often before people who know not one word of English, have carried the ideals and spirit of our heritage and democracy where America is only a distant fable.

"Motion pictures can have a tremendous effect both in this country and beyond our borders. They can portray the spirit and meaning of America in a way that nothing else can. But to do that we must seek and find the spirit within ourselves. The spirit of hope and vision. It is not the challenge of dollars – it is the challenge of ideals and ideas...It is what we do in the future that will effect the world. The potential force of motion pictures for good has just begun to be tapped. All we have done is only a foundation for future greatness. But we can take pride in that our foundation is a firm one. It is solid bedrock for future generations of pioneers to build upon." –Harry Warner

---

Harry Warner Speaking to the Boy Scouts

Hollywood Citizen News
DECEMBER 24, 1952

"You boys don't know how fortunate you are to live in America. My father was a slave in Poland. He brought his family to America so they could be free. He didn't bring us here to acquire wealth. He knew that wealth can ruin. He would have us worry first that we have a good reputation. Never be ashamed of what you do that is honest.

The conflict today is between people of faith and those who have none. It matters not whether one is a Jew, Catholic or Protestant. People of faith must stand united. Their foes seek to divide them, to cause them to fight among themselves so as them to conquer them..."

Our Film Folk

Harry Warner Speech
The California Jewish Voice
APRIL 3, 1953

When I was a boy, I sold papers and shined shoes to make two dollars to bring home so that my family could live. Then I was a shoemaker until I was twenty years old, and then I learned to be a butcher. My father, the best man who ever lived, taught me that I had to work for a living, and never expect anything from anybody. He was a great man, and I am proud to tell you, a very wise one. He taught me, 'Son, never look back. Never look back because the past has always been sad. There are so many things in everyone's life that makes them sad, so look forward!'

My father brought me to this country from Poland when I was six and a half years old. Today I am 71. But I'm going to fight! We here in America must stand and fight together, and we can defeat any dictator who tries to make us slaves. I can tell you that if you have all the money in the world, and not have a place to live as free human beings, you've nothing! We've got to fight! In the name of God, people must remember one thing: It doesn't make any difference what your faith is. The important thing is HAVE YOU GOT ONE? Together we can survive. Divided we must fall."

Warner Aids Campaign

The Herald
MAY 14, 1953

"Faith is not of one religion but is actually the premise on which all religions are based. Then the realization came to me that faith is not confined to any one religion. Our family came here to find freedom. And I was taught that if we had not been able to come here we would have perished. I know now that the debt never can be repaid.

Freedom cannot be bought: it must be earned; it cannot be paid for, except by preserving it for others to enjoy in the future."

The End

Jack talked to Harry about a group of investors he knew that wanted to buy the brothers out of their stock. Jack urged the sale of the studio, saying they had fought a long, noble battle, and now it was time to retire. Jack had already spoken to Abe, and he had agreed to sell as long as Harry went along with it.

Harry didn't want to let go. The studio and its employees were an extended family to him. He loved the work, the challenge of making great movies, as well as staying one step ahead of the competition, and looking into the future through the medium of film.

On May 11, 1956, it was written in a press release that "Working control of Warner Bros. has passed into the hands of a small group of investors headed by Serge Semenko, Senior Vice-President of the First National Bank of Boston, who on May 9th paid the brothers $22,000,000 (today's equivalent of $243,639,328) for 800,000 shares or 90% of the brothers' holdings."

Harry had at first rejected Semenenko's earlier offer to purchase his stock in February 1956, but later accepted the offer after Semenenko increased his bid and agreed to make the head of Fabian Enterprises, Simon Fabian, the new President of Warner Bros.

May 14th 1956, Louella Parson's column said, "All three brothers dined together at Perino's. About to sell the studio for over 22 million dollars, they could afford it."

May 31st 1956, a newspaper reported, "The Warner brothers themselves had a falling out and the only way Harry could be induced to sell his stock was via an offer for $30 a share compared to $27.50 a share.

Jack had made an under the table deal with Serge Semenko of the Bank of Boston, bought his 200,000 shares back, and anointed himself the President of Warner Bros.

Harry found out about Jack's dealings while reading an article in Variety magazine on May 31, 1956, and collapsed after reading the news.

While at the hospital, he suffered a stroke that impaired his walking ability and forced him to use a cane for the rest of his life.

July 11th 1956 press release, "Acquisition of a major portion of the stock held by Harry and Abe Warner was completed today. The revised set-up has Jack Warner as the President of the studio. He also retains substantial stock holdings in the company."

On July 11th 1956, the newspaper reported that Harry Warner had been admitted into Cedars of Lebanon Hospital in Los Angeles for "observation." (The report was not quite true—Harry had suffered another heart attack.)

When Betty, his daughter, went to visit him at the hospital, Harry told her he loved her and that she was a good person. They gave each other a hug. He then announced to the nurse that he was leaving the hospital and that he was going back to the ranch—his beloved ranch. He asked where were his pants? He got out of bed, and opened the closet. Two nurses put him back in bed and said they would call the doctor. Disgruntled, he agreed as along as he could go home that night.

He did go back home and enjoyed the ranch until he had to move closer to town as his doctor wouldn't drive out to the ranch anymore. Rea and Harry moved to a home in Bel Air in Los Angeles. He quickly deteriorated from there.

The Last Time
I Saw Grandpa

A guard opened the iron gate at the entrance of an old, austere Bel Air mansion with big columns flanking the front door. My mother and I stepped into this huge mausoleum of a house with shiny marble floors.

Why was Grandpa Harry here and not at his beloved ranch?

I listened for his greeting, but it didn't come. Instead, I was led down a long hall into a dark, antiseptic-smelling bedroom. The person stretched out on the bed was like a statue, not the vital, spirited grandfather I knew.

I heard the nurse say he had eaten a little, but that he was still unable to speak. She bent down close to his ear. "Mr. Warner, your daughter and granddaughter Cassie are here to see you." He gave no response.

A mysterious force drew me to him as if he were a candle in the dark. It was a gentle force.

His eyes were open, and moved to take me in. He smiled. I watched his hand inch slowly across the sheet toward me until it found mine. He tried to speak, but no words came. Instead, the look in his eyes did the talking. His hand tightened around mine, sealing the message—something special was being entrusted to me. I squeezed back. A promise was made.

He tried to sit up but was too weak. The nurse rushed over. I was being escorted out. I felt something tugging at me, telling me not to leave.

"Cassie."

I turned to look at him. He was reaching for me, but I was hustled out of the room. It was the last time I would see him.

I was ten years old then. It wasn't until years later that I would realize the magnitude and meaning of that moment.

Harry died at home on July 25, 1958 from a cerebral occlusion or stroke.

Eulogy

Rabbi Magnin spoke at Harry Warner's Funeral on July 27th 1958 at The Wilshire Boulevard Temple. Grandpa was taken to The Home of Peace Cemetery in East Los Angeles and buried in the family vault entombment.

Rabbi Magnin had this to say, "Some of us are closer to God than others, in sweetness, in kindness, in the humanities, and Harry Warner was one of those who was close.

There was never a kinder more humane individual than he. I know of philanthropists who love nobody, who give money, but not their hearts. Harry gave heart as well as money. He was one of the nobliest men I have ever known.

Harry Warner left an imprint, an impression on people, from those in top brackets to the poorest of actors. He also was a great American who appreciated America and gave to all Americans, regardless of race or creed. He will be remembered because he as a human being, a gentleman, and a good American."

Harry and Rea Warner

The Warner Family

by Harry Warner's Daughter Betty

Neither my mother nor father spoke to us about their origins—where they came from or what the old country was like.

My mother, Rea, came over on a boat from Manchester, England to America when she was 3 years old in 1891. She grew up in Shaker Heights, a suburb of Cleveland, Ohio.

Her father was British and her mother, Jennie Krieger Levinson, was possibly German as her mother's maiden name was Levinson. The Kriegers lived in Germany before WWII. Her mother, my grandmother, was a straight backed, prim, proud, and quiet lady who I never saw smile or touch anyone. She had high standards and felt she had achieved a certain intellectual level. They once were quite wealthy. They came to the U.S. because of the Nazis, and many came to Los Angeles. It was Grandma Levinson's family who was better educated, and had made more of a success, both financially and in being in the profession of: doctors, lawyers, businessmen, bankers, etc. Rea kept close watch over their well-being, and was very generous supporting them when it was necessary. I assumed Rea's father died when she was young, as he was never talked about. I know nothing about him.

Rea took great pride in her ability to remember numbers and often stated because of her ability to save money that the Warner brothers were able to start up their business, as she put the money they made in a safe place.

My mother was a beautiful young woman. She was 5'2" tall and weighed around 105 pounds. Her hair was black and abundant, and her brown eyes warm and expressive. Her chin determined, her face heart-shaped, and her nose slightly aquiline—with a prominent bridge which gives it the appearance of being curved or slightly bent. Her posture was elegant. She held herself erect and her head held high. Her waist was tiny.

Her body in proportion—her bust womanly and her hips small. Her skin was alabaster—soft and white. Her bones were small, her feet were small, and her hands thin and elegant.

She was proud that her weight and figure measurements stayed the same all her life. She took care of her physical well-being. Her skin being so fair prevented her from ever being in the sun without a hat or umbrella. She was corseted all her life. Her feet, in later life, were swollen with bunions, but she never wore low heels or unattractive shoes to accommodate the pain. She was not an athletic person. She played some golf with Harry.

Young Betty with Her Dad

When I was born in 1920, mom and dad started living in a double house—a two family home in Far Rockaway, a neighborhood on the eastern part of New York City, which they shared with dear friends, Harry and Bea Goetz and their two children. We shared this arrangement for at least a year or two. Dad was traveling to build up business mainly in Europe and then some in the Orient around the time I was born. Rea loved to travel with him, so they were gone a lot. I had a lot of love and warmth from a black maid, Beulah, the first couple of years of my life.

When I was three-years-old, Harry built a home on Rossmore Ave. in Los Angeles. We moved out to Los Angeles. This was a big change as the house was huge. The grounds seemed enormous as well. There was a pool, a tennis court, and a play yard. Each of us had our own room. For the first time, we had a dog—a German shepherd. The living room was the most formal room, and Rea had Lewis, Doris and myself as cherub angels painted on the ceiling with ribbons tied around our middle. We lived on Rossmore for 3 years. Mother also had a painting of herself in a beautiful blue velvet gown that hung in the living room. I had a portrait in a blue velvet dress, white lace collar, black Mary Jane shoes, and because sitting there was so boring I held and read a book, "Dr. Fu Manchu." It was exciting enough a book to keep me sitting quietly for the 12 sittings.

I remember going to The Vitaphone/First National studio in Hollywood on Sunset Blvd. There were several soundstages, and I fondly remember wandering around the back lot that was filled with outdoor sets, carpenter shops and rooms filled with furniture to use in the current films. There was also a place for boats or ships and false seas for the boat. There were huge painted back drops to create the illusion of location.

In 1926, we went back east again and we stayed there until 1936 when I was sixteen. From 1926 to 1936, we spent at least four or five months out in California every year on the beach in Santa Monica.

When we left Los Angeles, we moved to an apartment on the west side in New York City at 91st near the Hudson River. My memory is of a dark, small apartment with the halls, walls and furniture always smelling of food. There was a park on the river around the corner where Harry, my sister Doris and I would go horseback riding in Central Park on rented horses. They rode much better than I so I was left behind with a teacher. I had a governess who I hated, but I learned to speak French.

They learned to live well, as soon as they had money. Rea had an instinct for luxury living. It was natural to have servants and live in luxurious surroundings. Rea wasn't a self-conscious person. Caring how she looked was important, and she never failed to introduce herself as "Mrs. Harry Warner." She took on that identity with dignity and respect and she expected people to treat her as someone important, once her husband was successful. She was a very warm person. She liked people, and in everybody's mind they felt she was truly interested in them. She did best one-on-one.

Rea

As the wife of Harry Warner, Rea had a role to play in the community. She belonged to temple and hospital committees and gave money to Jewish causes. Both Rea and Harry were realistic about their roots. They never put on airs. They never did social climbing or did the party circuit. They didn't choose their friends because they had money. The friends they had were friends for a very long time. Rea was a loyal friend, and had the same friends for 40 or 50 years. She was firm, strong and positive. She had a sense of self-worth. She had a good head for figures and an excellent memory. She was polite, warm and straight. (She didn't play games with people.) She always said wistfully that if she had put her mind to a particular problem (in business) she would have been good at solving it.

I learned from this that you'd better get out there and do whatever you want to do. That it wasn't enough to play cards and have a comfortable social life, as I saw that this was not fulfilling her certainly. She did work at being a wife and mother. Being the wife of Harry Warner was a lot of work. She saved money and kept Harry in good spirits. She believed in him and was supportive—except for his gambling. Owing money drove her crazy. He shared a lot with her, but I think he kept a lot from her.

She loved living in a city, she liked traveling, seeing new sights and meeting new people. She was not a stick in the mud. Early on Rea and Harry traveled to Europe, Los Angeles, Philadelphia to her sister, to the horse races in Florida, Saratoga, etc. Harry loved to go if it had to do with business or gambling.

She was a strong family person, especially with us and her side of the family. She loved to entertain family and friends. She was the most comfortable with other Jews. She was not religious. She and Harry belonged to a reform temple and mostly went to high holidays—Yom Kippur and Rosh Hashanah. Jews treated her with respect befitting Harry's wife. They always sat in the first row at Temple. She was used to being the first in line, the first out, especially in restaurants. She loved going to the high holidays to be with friends and to show off her new outfit. She had a special one made each year for this occasion.

Harry and Rea never pushed religion on the family. He never lit candles on Sabbath. He celebrated both Christmas and Chanukah. We had Passover service and I went to Sunday school sometimes.

Rea never learned to drive. Harry never drove either, in my memory. He went to the office in New York with friends or by limo. He would come back to take Rea to lunch or go to the theatre or the opera in the evening. Rea loved the opera. Harry slept through every opera produced at the Metropolitan Opera House.

Rea also loved baseball, football, and ice hockey. When she got older she watched them on the television. She played cards with her friends, "The Girls" as they were known to husbands and families. She loved to read. She had many friends and children of her friends often came to her for advice.

She had a very high standard of proper behavior and dress. I must have driven her crazy with my tomboyishness, and disdain for her standards, especially in my dress and my aptitude for outdoor games—swimming, tennis, golf and rough housing were my favorite occupations. She was quite judgmental and didn't hesitate to let you know how she felt about our looks or behavior. She wasn't unkind verbally, but she said what she thought was correct. She nagged about one's appearance, especially posture. I was too thin as a kid and too noisy.

None of us played the piano—to everyone's dismay, I was not gifted. Even my music teachers needed infinite patience. I was rewarded with gold stars and pretty stickers to give me incentives to memorize my pieces. At

8 years old, I was a disaster at my first recital. I was not asked to perform publicly again, as I was bad advertising for the teacher.

I went to the local public school until my last two years of high school. They didn't want me to be snobby. Mt. Vernon was a suburban town. My friends lived in a middle-class neighborhood bordering our estate. I could walk to school and walk to my friend's homes.

Lewis played polo and we had a great painting of him dressed in a white shirt and pants, black boots with a polo mallet. He had played football at Columbia University until he broke his leg. His best friend was the quarterback, Ralph Hewitt, and for four years we went every Saturday during the season to his football games. The quarterback was my second hero—next to my brother. I often got to sit on the bench near the team.

Rea was an inveterate shopper, and most of her walking would be around shops. She dressed beautifully and her clothes were made in Paris or at a favorite designer in New York, when she had the means. She wore hats flatteringly and had a special hat designer. She never went out without a hat, gloves, shoes and matching handbag. Around the house, she wore silk lingerie and nightgowns also especially made. Her robes were silk or velvet or brocade. Her slippers or mules matched as well. She was extremely neat. Her hair was long and never worn softly down, but at leisure in the privacy of her bedroom, it would be in a single braid. Outside of her room, she wore it up. She was good with styling her hair, even though she went to a hairdresser once a week for a manicure, pedicure and styling. Her hair was never out of place. She was not high style but had very ladylike elegance. Her handkerchiefs had her initials on them and were trimmed with lace. She never accepted Kleenex as a substitute. She loved perfumes but not excessively. As they became wealthier, she had clothes for every occasion: outfits for golfing, at home, yachting, walking, day dresses for lunch with her friends and dinner dresses for evening events and ball dresses for the opera and special occasions. Her clothes were soft colors for day and were mainly beige, and navy or black for night. At night, she might include a green or sapphire blue gown. She loved crepes, velvets and chiffons. She also bought jewelry from a favorite jeweler friend in New York—diamonds, emeralds, rubies and pearls were her favorites. She had matching pins, earrings, bracelets and necklaces. Like everything she did, they were exquisite and never in poor taste. Harry paid the bills seemingly willingly. He wanted his wife to have the best. He was not good at giving gifts, so even on birthdays he would have his secretary pick out the gift or Rea would pick it out herself—a small thorn in her side.

Rea was the one who decorated or had her homes decorated. Harry couldn't care about such details. He, however, chose the location of their home.

Dad bought a twenty-two-acre property not even cleared of trees out in the country in Mt. Vernon, New York in 1926. Rea loved New York city, but Harry preferred the country. Rea wanted a large house and Harry wanted a farm filled with chickens, horses, cows, sheep, pigeons, cats and dogs. They both got what they wanted.

Rea loved a large entrance hall with marble and an imposing staircase. There was a powder room, a company closet, a formal living room, a library a breakfast room, a pantry, a kitchen, and a help's dining room. There was also a billiard room, a sun room, and downstairs a projection room that could also be used as a bowling alley when films weren't being shown, complete with small stage for party entertaining and family gatherings. Outside were stables for the animals, a pond for ducks and geese, chickens, a pasture for cows which later were turned into a 9-hole golf course with the cows still grazing and being hazards for the golf players. We had a small lake with an island in the middle, and the rowboat was much in use. In the winter, we could ice skate on the lake. There was sledding down the front driveway. There was a flagpole right near the house to catch the lightening. Doris hated storms so the flagpole was often the lightening rod.

Mt. Vernon was pretty self-sufficient. We had eggs, chickens, milk, butter, cream, squabs, ducks, and a few pheasants. There was lamb, beef, veal, calves liver and tongue served. The meals always included potatoes, vegetables, bread, salad and a rich dessert. Forever frugal despite being a multi-millionaire, dad would take the eggs he raised to the office to be cooked for lunch.

There was an Olympic-size pool, tennis courts, croquet grounds, and the sheep grazed on the large front grounds. There was also a riding ring, butcher shop, commercial refrigerator, a vegetable garden, grape vines for wine, a house for the head gardener, rooms for the chauffeur and other helpers, and a teeny house I could call my own.

In the house upstairs, each of us children had a bedroom and sitting room, a dressing room and bathroom. Rea and Harry had a huge bedroom, dressing room and bathroom. Lewis's suite was nearest to Rea and Harry's. He'd play music on his phonograph day and night—loudly. It drove them crazy. His rooms were done in elegant woods and very art nouveau-ish. His were the most modern rooms in the house. My bedroom was very simple with two beds, a bookcase and a night table. Not very interesting at all. Doris had matching bed covers for her two beds and curtains.

One wing held three guest rooms, a sleeping porch and two maid's rooms. There was a maid for mother to take care of her and her clothes, a cleaning maid, a male helper, who would also wait on tables. There was also a cook, who could make schneken and all kinds of pies. (Schneken is a German coffee cake with raisins, cinnamon and topped with a honey glaze.)

The house downstairs was built around magnificent rooms purchased from old mansions that had been torn down in New York. The paneling, the walls and fireplaces, floors and chandeliers were all purchasable and movable. I spent hours, when the folks were away dancing in the marble entrance hall. The sound was great.

Every Saturday and Sunday, Mom loved having a lunch and a dinner with 15-20 people. Many times, it was with relatives or friends. Dad loved to tell stories and jokes. It was a command performance. He had made his own wine with the help of an Italian gardener who lived on the property with his wife and child, and they became like family. Because I was young, I was allowed to invite one or two friends to come for dinner on the weekends. During the week Rea, Harry, Lewis and Doris would be in New York City in the evenings. I usually had a friend from school over.

Rea knew how to prepare a menu without ever stepping near the stove. When the help were off on Thursdays, I was allowed to go into the kitchen and cook my favorite meal—waffles with ice-cream covered in butterscotch sauce. Since the chef had to be a super baker, the breads, coffeecakes, pies, cakes and cookies were always there to be eaten.

They joined a reform temple in Mt. Vernon, New York, where we lived and were constantly angry by the constant money requests. They went to high holidays at the temple. We celebrated Purim, Rosh Hashana and Yom Kippur. The celebration dealt more with an abundance of food than the ritual. The rituals were meant to be hurried through so we could eat sooner.

Most of the group activities were in New York City. Going to the theatre was as popular as movies. They took me often, after which Harry, Rea and I would go to Schraffts restaurant for a special treat for me—a club sandwich, French pastry and a vanilla soda.

One Christmas, Lewis, gave me my own dog—a St. Bernard puppy that I called "Brando." I found Brando under the Christmas tree, and it was one of the loveliest gifts I ever got, and it made me love Lewis eternally. When the dog grew large, we had to have a handler for the shows as he would drag me around. Brando was lovable, and Rea allowed me to keep him in doors, even if he drooled and thought he was a lap dog. He'd backed up to several ladies and sit in their laps—covering them with his whole body. He would be temporarily exiled.

My brother, Lewis was 6 foot 1 inches tall, handsome, dark hair and eyes, long dark eyelashes, a strong nose which was broken when playing polo or football, a strong body, and well-coordinated. He was full of fun, and he was extremely sexy to the ladies.

Many times, Lewis was the catalyst for my parent's social life. He brought home his many girlfriends—some showgirls, and his boy friends from school, his theatre and night club connections, who first were from high school at Worcester Academy, a private school in Massachusetts that was founded in 1834, and later from Columbia University. The house was always open to all our friends. There was much hub bub, music on the phonograph, and someone playing the piano, and evenings of a buffet dinner and a movie down in the projection room. I remember Dick Powell, Joan Blondell, Ruby Keeler, and Al Jolson coming to the house for such evenings.

Lewis and his band of friends treated me like their mascot and included me when they went to football or ice-hockey games and later on to fraternity events. Two of them became my special friends, and one of them gave me his fraternity pin when I was 14 years old. They organized tennis matches, swim meets, touch football games and ping pong games. We had a small lake with an island in the middle, and the rowboat was much in use. In the winter, we could ice skate on the lake. There was sledding down the front driveway.

Lewis was being groomed to be the head of the studio. He had spent some time in California and Harry thought he was a natural. I think, Harry thought that he, Harry, could stay on in New York, if Lewis was in California. Lewis was one of the first to go to college. It was expected that after graduation he would go out to California.

Lewis was friendly with the Costello sisters and John Barrymore, and had come out with us to Hollywood to learn the business. It was Harry's idea that Lewis would help Jack run the studio. At this point, Albert was the only brother who was left in New York.

At age 21, Lewis graduated from college. Shortly after, he flew to Cuba with a girlfriend. Unfortunately, he had an unknown impacted wisdom tooth, and while in Havana developed a serious fever. Harry went down to fly him back to a U.S. hospital. Airplanes were not pressurized, and there were no antibiotics in those days. I saw him once in the hospital. His face was bandaged, but he was the same beloved Lewis. In his room were his two favorite girlfriends—one a brunette, Flora, and the other a lovely blonde, Gwen. I hated seeing him sick, and I didn't go back to see him again. The infection spread throughout his body, and in a few days, I was in my bedroom when I was told he had died! I cried alone for hours until Rea and Harry returned home. From then on, all our lives were different.

After Lewis passed away, no music was allowed. No weekend parties. Rea remained in her darkened bedroom often. Rea and Harry went often to Temple for solace. Rea spent some time with Aunt Rose, Harry's sister, in her New York apartment, with her sister Sally, for dinner or lunch but otherwise she mourned and we were asked to go about our life quietly. I was still allowed to have friends over, but her grief permeated the house. Doris was devastated. She became more rebellious and dated boys Harry didn't approve of. She spent a lot of time away from house with Lewis' two best girlfriends, Gwen and Flora. Luckily for me, I had many friends in the neighborhood and my social life with my peers took up the free time I had after school. I had become so used to having a full household, I didn't want or know how to be alone.

Doris went away to Washington DC to "finishing school." This changed my life, as she was my best friend—especially as an ally against our parents. After Lewis died, some of his friends stayed her friend and so they continued to come to the house. Rea and Harry enjoyed having them as a memory of Lewis.

In hindsight, it was lucky for me all this pressure and expectation was put on my sister, Doris, not me, after Lewis died. At first, she was being groomed to take Lewis' place, and be an executive in the business. She was intelligent, sharp and shrewd and had the requirements for a successful career, but she didn't like the pressure of having to live up to this. The mantle was too heavy. She did accept the role of "Princess," and wanted to use her title mostly for fun and games on the social scene. Plus, being a "woman" executive was not an acceptable job at that time.

I was permitted to be a normal child. I went to public schools, did athletic things like swimming and tennis. I had dates with my school boyfriends—went to the movie theatres, went out for hamburgers and sodas after. I might have felt neglected sometimes but being left to my own devices had many pluses. I knew I was loved. Dad always thought of me as his "sweet baby girl."

Rea's health was not robust. She had a lot of trouble with her pregnancy with me, a lot of trouble afterwards. I know she was always having stomach troubles. (I attribute some of it to the corsets.) She had gas and indigestion problems and was often constipated. She frequently took enemas and went to the doctor, for many years, at least once a week. Her personal diet of toast, Jello, dry chicken slices, and hot water with lemon never interfered with her having sumptuous meals for the rest of us.

She was stoic about her illnesses and never let out her pains on us. She still went out and did other social activities. She broke her ankle and another time her coccyx bone, but it didn't stop her. She traveled and went to the races with a rubber tube to ease the sitting.

The Warner family when they were together told Yiddish jokes and used Yiddish words and phrases. They never lost sight of their humble beginnings and their silence about the old country was a fierce desire to forget about the humiliation and physical threat that they suffered at the hands of the Cossacks. My father seemed relieved and truly proud to be in the United States. Another way of putting it was they were proud to be Jews and thrilled to be citizens of the U.S. Being Jewish was their religion which was separate from their citizenship in this land of opportunity, and relative freedom and justice. They were always aware of Anti-Semitism and wanted to change this attitude—not giving up their religious origins but becoming a part of American social and political proceedings. Many Jews felt becoming American liberals or radicals came from their Jewishness and their heritage, and from the oppression in the old country.

Harry became the patriarch of the family early on. He was beloved and respected and gave love, warmth and a joy of life to all. Ben thought of his children in tribal terms as well as did Harry. The family had to work together on all projects—from the butcher shop to the film business, especially the older boys. From the age of 7, he helped his father by selling newspapers, breaking in horses, and was taught to be a cobbler and then a butcher. He was self-educated and was street smart.

Grandpa Benjamin never made a lot of money. He loved playing pinochle and having fun. He had twinkly blue eyes and everybody liked him.

The Warner sisters came to dad for advice. Their husbands were taken in to the tribe and provided with jobs but given little respect.

My father was a workaholic, and seemed to have thought it was fun to work, and to work hard. I never saw any period of his life when work wasn't important to him. He was responsible for the family's good name and for the success or failure of "the business." He had no formal education and read but not for pleasure. He knew he had to be a straight arrow to gain the respect of a hostile American business community—a community of bankers and entrepreneurs who were not comfortable with Jews. His being a Jew was a fact in which he seemed to find a great deal of pride in his heritage and origins. He was pleased to be accepted by non-Jews, but cautious.

Ben Warner

My father was a loner and a very serious man. He was always very pragmatic, and he had a lot of dignity and strength. He felt good about himself and what he had achieved. The studio was his baby. It was his product and he was proud of it. It was up to him to provide the money and watch carefully what films were being made. He dealt with bankers constantly as the studio was in constant need of funds to continue productions.

He was extremely patriarchal about the people who worked for him. In other words, he took an interest in people who worked for him. He knew their names, their children's names, he knew when they were sick, knew when they got married, and what was going on everywhere. He was the benevolent boss. He enjoyed it. He was proud of it. He was proud of the way the studio looked. He was proud of the number of sound stages there were, and he was proud of the pictures that were made.

Harry loved being in America away from the pogroms or attacks against the Jews in his native country. The United States was the "land of opportunity." He often spoke of his responsibilities as a filmmaker and insisted on making films about the constitution and the founding fathers and people like Louis Pasteur, the conditions of the prison system, the underworld and other socially committed dramas.

Warner Bros. was successful because they had a sense of daring, and a sense of keeping in touch with what was going on in real life and around the world. They made movies taken from the headlines of newspapers which were topical stories.

Dad would go once a year with beautiful presentations of films they wanted to make or in many cases had already made to a stockholder meeting. The brothers would gamble on what the stockholders and the distributors wanted. Usually the annual stockholders meeting was in the dead of winter, so it was difficult for the stockholders to make it to the meeting. They were always planning a year ahead.

He hoped that the year before paid for the year ahead. When it didn't, dad had a genius for getting loans from banks. He would say, "Yes, we're in debt $2M, but last year's profits will come in in six to eight months, and we need money now for new films." He was always borrowing from the banks, and keeping the wolf from the door. He was wonderful at this. The people at the banks liked doing business with him. They felt he was honest, they were excited by the films and the picture business. It was a glamorous business and they liked to be involved in it. They trusted him.

I remember him as being a quiet man but very strong with very positive opinions and ideas. He had high integrity and was extremely honest in his business dealings, and he expected everybody else to behave in the fashion he required of himself, so he was really demanding of other people. He was kind. He was a straight shooter. He was just a very straightforward "this is who I am", and "you'd better be who you are." And if you weren't, he didn't like it, and he'd let you know. He spoke clearly as to what he wanted or how he felt about something.

He had been brought up from age six to take care of eleven brothers and sisters. He was the person who was supposed to be the breadwinner and find ways to make money, so he had a lot of responsibility all his life. So that's the way he lived his life—as a very responsible person. He loved to work—both at the office and at home. He was always busy. He didn't sit quietly for long periods of time. He could sit in a chair, take a 20-minute nap, and get up and go again. He was an energetic man. He loved construction and building.

Harry and Ben

He also loved going to studio parties in casual clothes. He hated tuxedos. He loved dancing, even though he was not a good dancer, as he was a little stiff, but he beamed the entire time he was on a dance floor.

As the head of the studio, one of his responsibilities was to open film exchanges for the distribution of Warner Bros. films all over the world. He spent much time in Europe, especially Berlin, and was well aware of what was happening with the rise of Hitler and fascism and Anti-Semitism. He warned those in the exchanges of these political changes and soon decided to close the exchange down so as not to do business with Hitler. He was the first company to do so, and he warned other American film companies of the political repercussions. No one listened and they continued to do business until the Germans took them over in 1936—banning all American films. When he returned to Hollywood, he expressed his concerns and encouraged Jack to make such films as "Confessions of a Nazi Spy," and "Mission to Moscow."

Harry and Jack

My father was a Democrat. Jack was a Republican. I recall the political atmosphere in the 1930s. They were both anti-Communists and isolationists. It took FDR years to bring business and the public around to acknowledging that Fascism might be as dangerous as communism which was destructive to our democracy—even though they saw Germany using Spain as a weapon testing ground. Premature anti-fascism was treated as pro-communism and was considered unpatriotic. In 1937, my father Harry was the first producer to make a definite decision on the course the industry would take during the war. There were 12 producers and supervisors producing 64 films in 1937.

Warner Bros. was a family company. It was owned and run by four brothers—brothers totally different in temperament and attitudes. They started making their own films in Astoria, New York so they could have material to show in the theaters they were acquiring. My father loved music, opera, the theatre and thought these were wonderful subjects to distribute on a mass basis. He always felt movies were supposed to educate as well as entertain.

One summer, when I was eight years old, he took me to Saratoga to the horse races. He was in debt $50,000 which was a lot of money. Not knowing if the horse was good or not, I thought the horse was good if its tail was up or it was grey in color. I picked eight winners in a row and got him out of this financial bind. I was invited to go to the races with him quite often after that.

After moving to California, Dad bought a 700-acre ranch in Calabasas, twenty miles from Hollywood where he lived and where the studio could shoot westerns. Later, he owned a 1,200-acre ranch in the San Fernando Valley where he found it relaxing to raise racehorses, livestock, and chickens. His grandchildren would come out to his ranch on Sundays, or he would come for Sunday brunch to their house, often entering by performing a soft shoe routine. He was as happy working on his farm or ranch as he was at the studio. Being outside with animals or a hammer in his hand or directing a tractor and driver or a trainer and race horse, building a fence, adding a room to his house made him a happy man. There was a big hill obstructing his view, so he bought a tractor and moved it. Dad had a lot of energy. He loved to get up at 6 in the morning, go to the barn and see a baby foal being born. This was one of the great joys in his life.

The Production Code

The Motion Picture Producers and Distributors of America (MPPDA, later called the Motion Picture Association of America) began in 1922 to 1960.

It spelled out what was acceptable and what as unacceptable content for motion pictures for a public audience in the United States. The office enforcing it was popularly called the Hays Office in reference to the President Will Hays.

The controversary surrounding film standards came to a head in 1929. A lay Catholic, Martin Quigley, editor of the Motion Picture Herald, a prominent trade paper, and a Jesuit priest, Father Daniel A. Lord, created a code of standards which Hays liked immensely, and submitted it to the studios. Lord was particularly concerned with the effects of sound film on children, whom he considered especially susceptible to their allure.

Several studio heads including Irving Thalberg of Metro-Goldwyn-Mayer (MGM), met with Lord and Quigley in February 1930. After some revisions, they agreed to the stipulations of the Code. One of the main motivating factors in accepting the Code was to avoid direct government intervention.

The Code was divided into two parts. The first was set of "general principles" which mostly concerned morality. The second was a set of "particular applications" which was an exacting list of items which could not be depicted. Some restrictions, such as the ban of homosexuality or the use of specific curse words, were never directly mentioned but were assumed to be understood without clear demarcation.

Its rules of "Don'ts" and "Be Carefuls" in 1927, were a set of guidelines that, among other things, said movies could not include:

- Pointed profanity meant by either title or lip—this included the words, "God," "Lord," "Jesus," "Christ" (unless they be used reverently in connection with proper religious ceremonies), "hell," "damn," "Gawd," and every other profane and vulgar expression however it may be spelled.

- Any licentious or suggestive nudity-in-fact or in silhouette; and any lecherous or licentious notice thereof by other characters in the picture.
- The illegal traffic in drugs
- Any inference of sex perversion
- White slavery
- Miscegenation (sex relationships between the white and black races) was forbidden.
- Sex hygiene and venereal disease
- Scenes of actual childbirth—in fact or in silhouette
- Children's sex organs
- Ridicule of the clergy
- Willful offence to any nation, race or creed
- The use of the American flag
- International relations (avoiding picturizing in an unfavorable light another country's religion, history, institutions, prominent people, and citizenry
- Arson; the use of firearms; theft, robbery, safe-cracking, and dynamiting of trains, mines, buildings, etc. (having in mind the effect with a too-detailed description of these may have upon the moron)
- Brutality and possible gruesomeness
- Technique of committing murder whatever method
- Methods of smuggling
- Actual hangings or electrocutions as legal punishment for crime
- Sympathy for criminals
- Attitude toward public characters and institutions
- Sedition
- Apparent cruelty to children and animals
- Branding of people or animals
- The sale of women, or of a woman selling her virtue
- Rape or attempted rape
- First-night scenes
- Man and woman in bed together
- Deliberate seduction of girls
- The institution of marriage
- Surgical operations
- The use of drugs

— Titles or scenes having to do with law enforcement or law-enforcing officers
— Excessive or lustful kissing, particularly when one character or the other is a "heavy."

Authority figures had to be treated with respect, and the clergy could not be portrayed as comic characters or villains. Under some circumstances, politicians, police officers and judges could be villains, as long as it was clear they were the exception to the rule. The entire document was written with Catholic undertones and stated that art must be handled carefully because it could be "morally evil in its effects" and because its "deep moral significance" was unquestionable. It was initially decided to keep the Catholic influence of the Code secret. A recurring theme was "that throughout, the audience feels sure that evil is wrong and good is right." The Code also contained an addendum commonly referred to as the Advertising Code which regulated advertising copy and imagery.

By the late 1960s, enforcement had become impossible and the Production Code was abandoned entirely.

Warner Family Tree

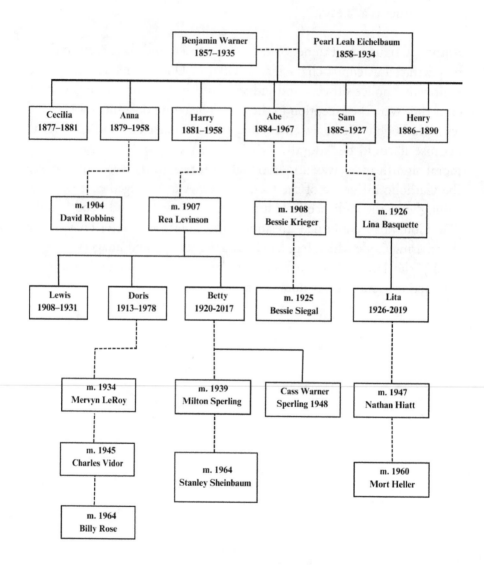

Benjamin Warner 1857–1935			**Pearl Leah Eichelbaum** 1858–1934		

Cecilia 1877–1881	**Anna** 1879–1958	**Harry** 1881–1958	**Abe** 1884–1967	**Sam** 1885–1927	**Henry** 1886–1890

m. 1904 David Robbins		m. 1907 Rea Levinson	m. 1908 Bessie Krieger	m. 1926 Lina Basquette

Lewis 1908–1931	**Doris** 1913–1978	**Betty** 1920-2017	m. 1925 Bessie Siegal	**Lita** 1926-2019

m. 1934 Mervyn LeRoy	m. 1939 Milton Sperling	Cass Warner Sperling 1948	m. 1947 Nathan Hiatt

m. 1945 Charles Vidor	m. 1964 Stanley Sheinbaum		m. 1960 Mort Heller

m. 1964 Billy Rose

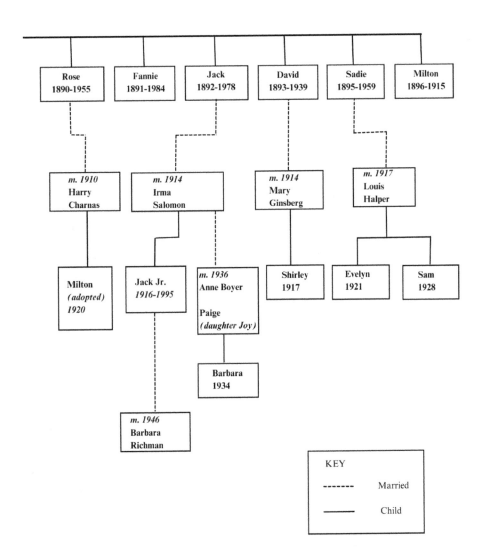

Rose 1890-1955	Fannie 1891-1984	Jack 1892-1978	David 1893-1939	Sadie 1895-1959	Milton 1896-1915

m. 1910
Harry
Charnas

m. 1914
Irma
Salomon

m. 1914
Mary
Ginsberg

m. 1917
Louis
Halper

Milton
(adopted)
1920

Jack Jr.
1916-1995

m. 1936
Anne Boyer

Paige
(daughter Joy)

Shirley
1917

Evelyn
1921

Sam
1928

Barbara
1934

m. 1946
Barbara
Richman

KEY

------- Married

———— Child

Acknowledgment

This book like any creative project involves kind souls who have cheered me on, and assisted where they could. I'd like to acknowledge them in the hopes that they too will feel pride in having participated in this labour of love.

I am especially grateful to my children (Tao Gaines, Cole Hauser, Vanessa Mooney, and Jesse Pool) for their many years of understanding about my passion for honouring those I care for with my time and efforts, and for them carrying on our beautiful legacy.

I thank my dear friend, Judy Code, and her stellar editing skills and contributions. I praise and appreciate Lisa Kastner for overseeing the production of this. Danny and Dani Kahn for being such supportive friends in so many ways. I appreciate Cindy Brokaw for her interest and assistance. My friend, Ted Adams, gave me the time and space to collect what I did when I initially got the idea to do this. My dear friend, writer extraordinaire, Howard Koch of Casablanca fame, encouraged me to tell the world about who my Grandpa was.

I'd like to include a future note of gratitude to the person or persons who support my next big dream—to tell my grandfather and the brothers' tale on screen and/or on television!

I'd like to throw out a big, warm wave of encouragement to others to believe in and nurture their dreams; and for having the dedication, intention, perserverance and smarts it takes to make one's ideas become realities!

To making this a better world with what we create; and to understanding and acknowledging those who make our lives rich with their love and caring!